T0283149

Praise for *Sticky, Sexy, Sad*:

"Midlife sex-positive feminist Treena Orchard takes us on a fascinating years-long anthropological adventure in which she hones her erotic knowledge with dozens of fascinating encounters with men (many of them much younger than her). In the process she becomes expertly attuned to the nuances of swipe culture and its messy and magnificent possibilities. Her head-spinning ride on the digital dating carousel is both exhausting and exhilarating as she valiantly seeks out the swipe of her life. I'm in awe of her unabashed lusty approach to life, love, and sex."

**Anne Bokma, author of *My Year of Living Spiritually:
One Woman's Secular Quest for a More Soulful Life***

"Treena Orchard's experience as an anthropologist helps readers make sense of our current reality of incessantly swiping in a world fed by instant gratification and algorithms. *Sticky, Sexy, Sad* is also a brilliant treatise on modern dating as a person in recovery and the challenges that recovery presents in a booze-soaked dating world. If dating app swipe culture makes you feel disposable and you want to understand why, read *Sticky, Sexy, Sad* by Treena Orchard."

**Tawny Lara, author of *Dry Humping: A Guide to Dating, Relating,
and Hooking Up without the Booze***

"Reading *Sticky, Sexy, Sad*, I found it hard to keep a smile off my face. Peering into the private reflections of someone's online dating world felt voyeuristic but was also tremendously fun. Squinting through one eye, worried for the author about the next unwanted dick pic story but then relaxing into the engaging storytelling, I think the author has done a wonderful job describing the often online search for modern love."

**Nora Loreto, author of *Take Back the Fight: Organizing Feminism for the
Digital Age, Spin Doctors: How Media and Politicians Misdiagnosed the
COVID-19 Pandemic,* and *From Demonized to Organized: Building the New
Union Movement***

"In a digital age dominated by dating apps, *Sticky, Sex, Sad* emerges as a timely exploration of the profound impact these platforms have on our lives. This groundbreaking autoethnography explores the intricacies of swipe culture and cracks open the landscape of love, sex, and romance in the twenty-first century. It is a must-read that challenges us to question how these apps shape the very essence of our connections."

Kaitlynn Mendes, co-author of *Digital Feminist Activism:*
Girls and Women Fight Back against Rape Culture

"Profoundly honest and oddly hopeful, Orchard's memoir is an honest foray into the sultry, sloppy, and downright stupefying world of swipe culture. Whatever you're looking for – validation, commiseration, a good laugh, or a stiff kick in the pants toward love – you'll find it here."

Lisa Wade, author of *American Hookup:*
The New Culture of Sex on Campus

"Treena Orchard's *Sticky, Sexy, Sad* is a captivating exploration of modern dating that blends vulnerable storytelling with insightful commentary on technology, desire, and consent. As a family doctor focused on women's sexual and mental health, I found the book's honest narrative both enlightening and profoundly relevant. It is an essential guide for anyone navigating the complexities of relationships in the digital age."

Sheila Wijayasinghe, physician and medical expert on *The Social*

Sticky, Sexy, Sad

Swipe Culture and the Darker Side of Dating Apps

Treena Orchard

ÆVO UTP

Aevo UTP
An imprint of University of Toronto Press
Toronto Buffalo London
utorontopress.com

© Treena Orchard 2024

ISBN 978-1-4875-4930-5 (cloth)
ISBN 978-1-4875-5114-8 (EPUB)
ISBN 978-1-4875-4993-0 (PDF)

Library and Archives Canada Cataloguing in Publication

Title: Sticky, sexy, sad : swipe culture and the darker side of dating apps /
    Treena Orchard.
Names: Orchard, Treena, author.
Description: Includes bibliographical references and index.
Identifiers: Canadiana (print) 20230587615 | Canadiana (ebook) 20230587623 |
    ISBN 9781487549305 (cloth) | ISBN 9781487551148 (EPUB) |
    ISBN 9781487549930 (PDF)
Subjects: LCSH: Online dating. | LCSH: Mobile apps – Social aspects. |
    LCSH: Love. | LCSH: Intimacy (Psychology) | LCSH: Sex.
Classification: LCC HQ801.82.O73 2024 | DDC 306.730285 – dc23

Printed in Canada

Jacket design: Kathleen Lynch/Black Kat Design
Jacket illustration: "Cereus, Queen of the Night," c. 1744 (hand-coloured
engraving), Georg Dionysius Ehret (1710–1770). The Stapleton Collection/
Bridgeman Images.

We wish to acknowledge the land on which the University of Toronto Press
operates. This land is the traditional territory of the Wendat, the Anishnaabeg,
the Haudenosaunee, the Métis, and the Mississaugas of the Credit First Nation.

University of Toronto Press acknowledges the financial support of the
Government of Canada, the Canada Council for the Arts, and the Ontario Arts
Council, an agency of the Government of Ontario, for its publishing activities.

Canada Council Conseil des Arts
for the Arts du Canada

ONTARIO ARTS COUNCIL
CONSEIL DES ARTS DE L'ONTARIO
an Ontario government agency
un organisme du gouvernement de l'Ontario

Funded by the   Financé par le
Government   gouvernement
of Canada   du Canada

Canadä

MIX
Paper | Supporting
responsible forestry
FSC® C016245
www.fsc.org

This book is for my mom, who taught me how to tell the hardest story: the truth.

I think the sheer fact of women talking, being, paradoxical, inex-
plicable, flip, self-destructive but above all else *public* is the most
revolutionary thing in the world.

– Chris Kraus, *I Love Dick*

Contents

Foreword by Dr. Wednesday Martin   ix

Introduction   1

1 Selfies for Days   21

2 Sex in Swipedom   64

3 Feminish   98

4 Copy & Paste   138

5 Love Me Tender   178

Conclusion   211

Acknowledgments   227

Bibliography   233

Index   241

Foreword

Since Darwin, field scientists, including anthropologists, have been fascinated by sexual behavior – social bonding, courtship, and mating – across species and cultures. Maybe this is because we are keen to understand our very own motivations, backstories, and futures when it comes to intimate connection. From Bronisław Malinowski's *A Diary in the Strict Sense of the Term* to Sarah Hrdy's *The Woman That Never Evolved* to Brené Brown's *Atlas of the Heart*, we've turned to works by narrators who blend scientific insight with personal revelation to help us understand why we feel what we feel, do what we do, and want what we want.

From the moment she redefines the dating apps that people in search of companionship cannot avoid as a new, strange, and seemingly limitless culture in the palm of our hands, Treena Orchard plants a stake in the ground. What makes *Sticky, Sexy, Sad* so important and surprising is that it manages to both update and upend a long tradition of academic inquiry into what makes us tick, sexually speaking. But it's also in how she does it. Dr. Orchard lays bare what it means to be (in the words of Sarah Hrdy) a strategic, facultative, continuously sexually receptive female *Homo sapiens sapiens* living in multiple, overlapping, contemporary ecologies: digital dating, sobriety, academia, Canada, and patriarchy among them.

Orchard describes the possibilities, passions, and pitfalls of being on Tinder, Bumble, and other apps from learning to become an adept sexter, to managing a man who tells her she looks like she combed her hair with an eggbeater, to navigating a date that shades into sexual coercion. This storyline would have been enough to keep us turning the page. But as an endlessly curious, courageous, and open-minded Everywoman with a doctorate turning the lens on herself and her online adventures, Orchard reveals powerful, poetic, and deep truths about desire, agency, and what it means to be a person who identifies as a woman with a libido in the first half of the twenty-first century.

If you're dating or have ever dated, if you know anyone who dates, if you have ever found yourself bewildered by your desires or the people you desire, *Sticky, Sexy, Sad* will delight you, educate you, and make you feel more connected to the humans you know and the ones you don't.

Wednesday Martin, PhD

Introduction

In a galaxy where men pull at women like the earth pulls at the moon, I stroke and seduce with such regularity that I must be good at it. Am I from Venus or from Mars? People fall into my untamed orbit on airplane rides, at parties, in bars, across crowded rooms, and while determining my academic future. I crash up against and allow so many bodies inside my own that it all seems quite natural. This is my cosmos.

There's more to the story, though. Wild luck or chance don't magically create these encounters. They're the determined work of the demons who stream through my blood and plant their crops in my scalp. Trauma is the ultimate squatter. It blows dark energy into my mother's advice about what happens between my legs and waters the soil of addiction. It also transforms my vulnerability into a superpower I use to lure people into my gleaming trap.

But it's not really mine, nor is it gleaming. It is a faulty structure created by men who hold the four corners of the earth at their mercy as the patriarchy is swallowed by rising waters. Men who force girls down back alleys and never stop to wonder what they are thinking or how old they are. Men whose bro code is international. We're drowning in the ocean, and yet they continue to scuttle up and down my shores like crabs feeding under a lunar glow.

How are you so wise? Where did you come from? Men playfully wonder while imagining my mouth on them. They wind themselves around me and gather at the foot of my bed to figure out how they got here. Years ago, steeped fully in the cups of alcohol, I'd laugh and say that my memoir would be called Of Vice & Men. *Oh the adventures that would fill those pages.*

But it wouldn't just document the hilarious hookups. It would also include terrifying blackouts and the sex I didn't understand or always want. The pleasure of honing my erotic knowledge and other beautiful things I never told anyone would also be nestled in its pages. This is not that story, but it honors the girl-woman who swims against the current of sexism and struggles to capture her voice in a society set on silencing women from freely speaking.

The girl is me, and maybe she is also you. I am learning to hold the door open for new ways of doing love, healing, and relating to people on this spinning orb we call home. Dating apps have foiled and fostered these primal aims. I'm not alone in this. There are millions of smart, funny, hot, weird, lonely, and confused people using these complex circuitries without a way to make sense of what their experiences mean. Until now. Let's discover what these platforms reveal about sexuality, dating, and our digital selves in the age of swipe culture.

The shivers and stings of sex, men, and intimacy shape my life. Sometimes happily so, but most relationships implode within weeks or possibly a year or two if we hang on that long. It's usually my fault, which is both true and false. My actions and decisions are my own, but they're also expressions of the complex forms of love and trauma I inherit from my family. The sexism and patriarchy that encompass the world around me impacts my relationships too. Mounds of therapy and a commitment to living a sensual life that reflects what I want and who I am as a healing woman is helping reset my relationship compass.

Dating apps play a central role in this process. That might seem like an obvious thing to say because they're how "everyone" meets nowadays, but for a lifelong Luddite like me it's extraordinary. What's also unthinkable is how hard dating apps kick my ass. Unthinkable because I've been up against some very formidable life challenges, heavy drinking and risk-taking to the point of self-annihilation among them. Yet these platforms crack me open in unanticipated and productive ways. The book you're holding is evidence of this.

I'm an anthropologist who studies sexuality; however, my swiping adventure does not begin as a research project. It starts with me very reluctantly downloading a dating app after a self-imposed period of celibacy following an abusive relationship. I enter Swipedom in August of 2017 when the effects of the #MeToo movement are beginning to ripple across the globe. Writing emerges as a way to manage the chaos and the compelling things I experience while swiping my way into new bodies and witnessing the realignment of feminism, sexual rights, and gendered advocacy.

Four months after my first swipe I've got 60,000 words written, and that's when I know a book is being born. The chapters shape-shift over time, but what counts as dating and what it feels like to inhabit these platforms drift to the top early on. So does an interest in excavating the swipe culture that engulfs and gives meaning to dating apps. Swipe culture refers to the social behaviors and the meanings we attribute to them as we swipe our thumbs across tablets, phones, and other devices. It's how we say "hello," "turn on," "yes," and it's dramatically altering the landscape of sexuality and dating.

Objectification, bro culture, and the gamification of romance are features of dating apps that have been explored at length. There are so many fascinating issues to dig deeper into and almost as many perspectives to take. This book is designed around the following questions: How do we learn to swipe? How are these apps impacting sex? What other functions do they serve? What are the feminist implications of surrendering to swipe culture? Can we navigate these choppy digital waters with dignity and find ways to feel empowered?

A Luddite Goes Digital

As a freewheeling feminist with a penchant for hands-on human interactions, using an app for anything other than checking email, taking pictures of my cats, or perusing the filtered mirage of Instagram is a massive stretch. I've never taken a computer course and know virtually nothing about how they work despite being entirely dependent upon them. When the Wi-Fi temporarily cuts out at home, it sends me into a frantic tailspin. Classic Gen X, I guess.

In Grade 10 I learn to type on a manual typewriter. I dread going to and from the "Intro to Business" class, held in the senior wing of our high school, a foreign land of party people with huge hair who look very old. Sporting acid-wash stirrup jeans and angular pastel sweatshirts, my hands poised in mid-curl above the machine, I anxiously wait for the teacher to yell "GO." In one-minute intervals we pound away on the keys, swish the carriage return, and compete with one another for higher word counts. I'm not great at it, but the frenzy of the keys as they walk onto the page and transform it from blank to black is sort of thrilling.

Eleven years later when I begin my PhD, I do not have a typewriter or computer of my own. So, in true neolithic style, I write out my thirty-page essays by hand on yellow legal pads. Then I hit the university computer lab to type them out on huge Frankenstein machines that are that plastic beige color reserved for things like radiator covers and stackable classroom chairs. When I finally get my own computer a couple of years later, I'm clueless about its inner workings and use it like an electronic typewriter. My ignorance when it comes to technology brings to mind the Beastie Boys' song "Shake Your Rump," which talks about Stone Age dude Fred Flintstone using his feet instead of wheels to drive his car.

Technology is clearly not my thing. But maybe that's not entirely true because, theoretically, technology is the application of scientific knowledge for practical goals and the products or tools that make these goals happen. Fire and the printing press, for instance, are considered technologies that have radically transformed human life. I'm definitely into those things, but less so the digital gadgets, smart anything, and apps other than Word or PowerPoint on my laptop. I've never once asked Siri to do anything for me.

The one spicy exception in my stone-age timeline comes in the early 2000s, when I have a brief rendezvous with online dating if you can call it that. The site I'm talking about is called Craigslist. You read that right. During my sad party days, tipsy on some Yellow Tail Cabernet, my libido hungrily scrolls the "NSA" or "no strings attached" section. If m4w28 or Hot Fun With You is available, we meet up. It's definitely a yard sale of people and pleasures, but scoring is easy.

For the next ten years I run down an increasingly dark tunnel of sex, love, and self-abandon until the spring of 2012, when I land with a thud at the bottom. It does exist. Relief and terror wash over me for the shaky first months, which I ride out with the man I've been seeing for some time. He also quits drinking for a while but opts out of individual counseling. In this relationship, characterized by gnawing anxiety and abusive trauma response patterns, smiles are as fleeting as dusk. But on my own, in the quiet rooms of my apartment and the grueling therapy sessions I never miss, things are spooling open, and I gather the courage to leave.

After a year of celibacy and another futile year of trying to rekindle old flames on the downlow, it hits me that I have no idea how to meet new men or how to do intimacy without substances. Instructions for addressing these dilemmas aren't included in the sobriety merch bag and it's not as though relationships, or anything for that matter, is the same as it was before. The universe is being turned inside out, and

I fall through the starlit ebony sky a changed woman, newly charged and ready for romantic exploration. Primed for action but out of familiar options, I'm forced to consider something that's exciting and mortifying. It's one thing to advertise myself and scroll the internet for strangers when I'm half in the bag, less so when I'm alcohol- and drug-free and rusty in the boudoir. Plus, isn't the whole online thing still embarrassing?

I take a massive breath, set my pride adrift, and sign up with Match.com because advertisements for this site keep popping up on my social media platforms. The guys look sort of basic and attractive, entry-level dating at its best. Elite Singles piques my interest too, and I wonder if men with money are any different than the economically challenged guys I normally gravitate to. I quickly learn that they're mainly divorcees who lie about their age, fawn over anything I say, and after three messages one fellow asks, "Hi, do you marry me?"

Give me those trashy nights on Craigslist any day! My one-month online dating life generates one marriage proposal, one scheduled date that never happens, and a horrendous one that actually does. Memorable for all the wrong reasons, this date is the first online experience that I write about. As this segment of the story, published in *The Chorus*, makes clear, there can be a great deal of confusion between how people perform on dating apps and how they act in real life:

As I made dinner, I glanced at him out of the corner of my eye, trying from as many perspectives as my optic design as a human would allow to make sense of what I was seeing. I was trying to assemble the pieces of a disappointing puzzle that was coming apart before me. If I looked hard enough, could I see the hot guy in the picture? Are you in there?

Could I see how women could love him and find him desirable?
What kinds of women have loved him, I wondered? I found myself
comparing him to a fun-house mirror, which reflects illusions. He
departed in every way from the ideas I had constructed. Was I com-
municating with two men, the guy inside the photo and the one press-
ing letters on a phone? Which one was leaning against the arch of my
kitchen, anxiously gulping red wine and talking about his exes?

Thinking that the desktop platform approach was the problem, I decide to bite the bullet and try a dating app on my
phone. Be modern, Treena, just do it. Gulp. But which one?
Tinder is supposedly for hookups, which I'm not against
but don't necessarily want to start with. Zoosk, a weird
word that reminds me of Zeus, an old guy tossing lightning
bolts in the sky, doesn't do it for me. Bumble is rumored to
have better-looking, more professional guys and its sleek
aesthetic gives it a more polished vibe than the others.

I'm intrigued by the promises of dating equity and female
empowerment through its signature format, in its hetero version,
as an app whereby women make the first move and ask men
out. In a 2015 *Vanity Fair* interview with Leora Yashari, Bumble
co-founder and former CEO Whitney Wolfe Herd describes the
app as "100 percent feminist," which generates loads of social
media buzz and over 100 million users worldwide. As a feminist, I see this app as the obvious choice. Can Bumble turn the
tide and offer the fun sex and good times I tell myself I'm ready
for? Will these things feel empowering? Can I actually learn to
use an app? Is sober romance fun? Am I ready for this?

Scrolling through my phone looking for sexy profile pictures is an exercise in self-defeat – all my body shots are of me
50 feet away and fully clothed. I look so wholesome! I don't
know any of these men and have never done this before, so

it's hard to imagine what they will be interested in. Also, what to include in my write-up, other than cats and reading are the best? After selecting some decent photos and a write-up that is far too long, I press the yellow "create" button.

OMG, I've done it. My phone sits face down on the mid-century modern coffee table a few feet away as the seconds drip by. Clueless about how the algorithm works or what's actually going to happen, I imagine a banquet hall of men milling around inside the device. Dressed in business casual, they engage in inaudible small talk amongst themselves. I can't see their faces and then I notice that instead of flesh and blood, they're made of paper. They drift around the room, light as feathers and identical in shape. Is this what it will be like?

I grab my phone and make my first swipe into the unknown. A left followed by a few more lefts and then a right. Men's faces appear one after another inside sunny circles of possibility. I observe them very closely, like my stepmom reading the tiny nutritional labels on food packages before she got LASIK surgery. Who are these people? Would I ever meet or see them outside my phone? It's so weird and almost magical that for a minute or two I wonder if they're even real.

But then the words "It's a match," in bouncy cursive yellow, pop across my screen. My stomach flips, and I feel dumb, scared, and galaxies out of my league. I don't know how to do this. Dating apps have been around for a few years at this point, so asking someone how to use them is way too embarrassing. You just swipe, right!?

As a medical anthropologist who studies sexuality, gender, and health, I document how other people live and the cultural environments that shape their experiences. I've interviewed and lived with women, men, and trans people involved in sex work, folks impacted by HIV/AIDS, urban and rural Indigenous populations, and sexual and gendered minority groups from across the world. Each project requires a unique approach to relationship building and often begins with a hearty dose of excitement and culture shock.

The same sense of discombobulation surfaces when I first swish my thumb across a dating app. This platform is a new cultural environment for me and instead of being located across an ocean or in a new city, it's sitting in the palm of my hand. Very meta, but also very Alice in Wonderland. There's no background notes or information to guide me through the digital rabbit hole I'm tumbling into. I have only my own life for context, that and my devastatingly dull digital tech skills. Will anyone want to date me? Am I too old? Who do I talk to about my experiences? Will I succeed?

It's like a thousand balloons have been released into the sky, destination unknown.

I want to master dating apps because I'm craving connection and want to be touched by someone new. Someone to whom I'm an entirely fresh story. I need to master these apps to see if all my healing work is doing the trick in terms of reconfiguring how I relate to and think about sex, men, and myself. Within days, all kinds of weird and wonderful discoveries surface. Carpe diem. Ziplining. Man with fish. Reordering priorities. Constant checking. Forced schmoozing. Disappearing acts. These observations flurry inside my head like tiny cue cards. Documenting this unfamiliar setting becomes an obsession and I'm the perfect person to do it. I know nothing about the apps and I'm skilled in the study of sexuality.

This writing project helps me navigate the riptide of feelings I'm immersed in, among them a sense of being lost, confused, turned on, and super vulnerable. It's also driven by my scholarly spidey senses that have been bleeping on high alert since my first swipe.

There's a lot going on inside my phone, much more than what appears in most online stories and even the academic research about dating apps. They're not just pathetic digital meat markets that bank on misogyny. It's more than deception and dick pics. There are loads of people leaning into one another in ways that seem counterproductive, mean, creative, and exciting, sometimes all at once. These responses are common enough to suggest that they're shaped by the design of the app itself.

My scholarly expertise in fact-finding in unfamiliar places comes in handy as I descend into this mysterious world. Only full-scale cultural immersion will do. What's also useful is my colorful and heart-clutching love life from the time before smartphones, which I use as a divining rod to assess, culturally and in a personal sense, what is happening in the digital romance matrix. Make way for the analog days.

My Backstory

A Gen Xer born in 1972, I grew up in an era dominated by corduroy, avocado bathtubs, Freshen-Up gum, and a kaleidoscope of musical influences that included the Bee Gees, David Bowie, Stevie Wonder, Queen, Joni Mitchell, and the Eagles. The women's movement is in full swing, and divorces are becoming more common, which really impacts family dynamics as well as the kinds of relationships kids see around them. My parents divorce after three years of marriage, and I spend my early childhood with my mom and stepdad. My dad comes back into the picture after a few years spent working in factories, farming, and various hippie endeavors. During the years that we get reacquainted he has several sandal-wearing, creative girlfriends, some of whom I meet; I always think they are pretty.

In 1979, my mom, my stepdad, and I move from our basement apartment located next to the freeway to a modest bungalow in the suburbs. The following year my twin sisters are born, and life changes a lot in our blended family. Visits with my dad on Sundays are cherished occasions that allow me to spend time in a calmer environment. He interacts with political, artistic, feminist people of different religious and racial backgrounds and I get to know these people's kids, some of whom are being raised communally and get to pick their own names. How cool.

At home, I'm often called upon to parent my sisters, manage the house while my stepdad is working out of town, and serve as a confidante to my mom, who begins drinking to cope with her loneliness. When she drinks she unspools the things that happened to her as a child in that big farmhouse on the hill. She is one of twelve kids in a rural Pentecostal household where speaking in tongues and quieting any talk of abuse was enforced. No wonder she was so sad.

I'd hear her say how ugly, fat, and worthless she is and think, in my child brain, that the same must be true of me. She wants to recede as far as possible into the places that offer a sliver of relief and invisibility. I do too. She also instructs me to be wary of men "who are only after one thing." These words make me afraid and also curious about men. They also make me feel like there's something inside me, the thing they want, that I need to fear. She's going to put me "on the Pill" as soon as I get my period. Who says I want to have sex? As a young girl with no desire to enter the world of adulthood, which seems a pretty complicated, sad place populated by messed-up relationships, sex and boys are the furthest thing from my mind.

I feel adrift between these competing worlds, too soon an adult in one and a temporary resident in the other. Edging into adolescence, I long for things to make life easier or more normal. One of them is the shiny mushroom haircuts that my straight-haired friends wear. I always imagine the lives of the girls who wear this bouncy, carefree style to be less tangled than mine. I also begin longing for someone to like me. I secretly pray to Ouija boards at sleepovers and when we play spin-the-bottle in treehouses. I make wishes to God before going to bed. Please, someone, like me.

One Friday night at our local Teen Club, when I'm twelve years old, I dance to "Drive" by the Cars with a new addition to our class, Miguel. As the song ends, he asks me out and I say yes. Our courtship consists of a visit to a nearby mall where I awkwardly ignore him because I think that's what you are supposed to do. After a couple weeks, I receive a phone call from a classmate who informs me that Miguel wants to break up with me. This call arrives on the only phone in the house, conveniently located in the kitchen where my family sits at the dinner table. With my back to them, I nod and say "I thought so," before slinking back to my plastic floral chair at the table while silently imploding with shame.

Grade 11 is a pivotal year because it's when I finally get my braces off and begin to muster some confidence about myself. A cute guy from the nearby Catholic school asks me out, and we date for a couple of months. I know him from track and field and had been admiring his fine freckled features for some time. In the yellow bedroom of the bungalow that he lives in with his family, our second- and third-base sexual activities proceed with steady heat. He wants to have sex and always has a condom in his back pocket whenever we fool around, but I'm not quite ready.

The final year of high school is the most fun. I make a decisive transition from low-key loser social circles to the elite group of naughty but preppy-looking girls. Very John Hughes. On a Friday night towards the end of the school year we're at a party on the east side of Saskatoon, drinking fast and making plans for later. I am seventeen and no longer want to be a virgin. It feels as simple as that, and I sleep with a guy at the party. I know him from the summer before when we made out and I got gum in my hair, which I tried to get out with ice cubes and peanut butter. The sex isn't painful and along with a sense of accomplishment, the experience feels powerful.

The news spreads like moralizing wildfire through the high school hallways, but I don't care. I view the sex as a progression in my life as a sexual person and in terms of having sex the way I want to. I'm not looking for a boyfriend but yearn to be loved or even liked. On the way to the bar, decked out in overalls or a vintage shirt with huge paisley patterns on the drapey sleeves, I hang out of the front seat window of my friend's car belting out lines from Linda Ronstadt's 1974 classic "When Will I Be Loved?"

Although I attract a lot of attention, relationships remain transient. I feel unlovable and completely ill-equipped to stay afloat in anything serious. Brief encounters are the order of the day for me and many of my friends. My pattern is often to cheat on guys when I'm drunk and act in other ways that ruin things. I have no clue what meaningful or healthy intimacy looks or feels like, and because it sort of scares me I repel it. Some nights, especially after particularly toxic or embarrassing experiences, I ride my bike for hours along the river. I look at the water, which curves ever so slightly in a long S shape, and make solemn promises to not get out of control again. I stay there for hours watching the water glide swiftly by and listening to the piercing cry of the seagulls swooping overhead.

Today going to counseling is common, but in the 1990s intergenerational trauma and addictions aren't really discussed and female sexuality is seen as a slippery mixture of danger, excitement, and trouble. I'm caught inside these overlapping cultural spaces as a messed-up young woman seeking validation through precarious means and as an

independent young woman exploring the powerful pleasures generated through sex and men on my own terms.

In *The Misfit's Manifesto*, Lidia Yuknavitch calls these
experiences portals instead of mistakes or failures. Without
these painful passageways we wouldn't have the capacity to
change, which is essential to finding a version of ourselves
that we can learn to love. These early years are an aching tale
of what it's like being raised by a woman who used tough love
to try to protect me the best way she could from the many terrible things done to her. They're also a record of my attempt
to live an interesting life inside a judgmental culture that lays
down hypocritical rules about sex, relationships, power, and
autonomy to women, men, and diversely gendered people.

Is it any surprise that I excel in a profession that is about
immersing myself in the lives of the socially excluded? Mis-
fits find each another. When someone in my research projects
talks about addictions or feeling neglected as a child, I don't
just tilt my head to the side and say, "Oh, that must have
been terrible." I know those things and communicate this
through sharing some of what I've gone through. Holding
the space together develops trust and rich insights. There is
communion in the act of hugging a woman after a powerful
interview or nodding to the old men who walk the streets
endlessly to stave off the numbing boredom of poverty.

I'm learning many things during my metamorphosis as a
healing woman, especially the importance of courage. You
can't love yourself without it. There is always a thread, like a
living rhizome connecting what we do with who we are, that
stretches far, far back. As Melissa Febos says in *Body Work*, "you
make the past known in order to know yourself as changed."

The Book

This book is like that. It's a way of reaching into the digital landscape and the soft warm flesh of what came before to make sense of things we share in the here and now. A desire to connect and test the waters of love, sex, kink, friendship, fantasy, whatever it is that rests on the horizon. Through the dual lens of a sexuality scholar and a woman seeking some sexy time, I explore the emotional circuitry that lights us up and leaves us stranded at the digital wayside when we swipe. My experiences as a cis, mainly heterosexual, woman seeking to date men dominate these pages, but I hope the book will resonate with people who identify within the range of sexual orientation and gender identity spectrums.

Using the researcher's life as subject of inquiry is called autoethnography. It's an established research approach that combines documentation with creative or literary techniques, memoir, and cultural critique. Autoethnography is about articulating insider knowledge of certain cultural experiences of which the researcher is a participant. A uniquely insightful way to speak against or provide alternatives to taken-for-granted ideas, autoethnography often complements and addresses gaps within the existing research. *Return to Laughter: An Anthropological Novel* by Eleanore Smith Bowen, *Voluntary Madness: Lost and Found in the Mental Healthcare System* by Norah Vincent, and *My Life with the Chimpanzees* by Jane Goodall are some fine examples.

Writing this book while also trying to get lucky in love has been grueling. Sticky notes with things like "2 expired

opening conversations," "6 matches," "2 app-to-phone texting," "GHOSTED" flutter throughout my house as I morph
from caterpillar to butterfly. Coffee-stained, stickered Mole-
skin notebooks filled with thoughts scatter my bookshelves.
Word documents and file folders bulge with thousands of
words, links, and resources. My five months on Bumble are
the most rigorously recorded because everything is new and
noteworthy. Over time, the notes are less detailed and more
thematic, which reflects how my dating life has transitioned
from a pseudo-experiment into the more meaningful and
embodied experience I desire.

The issue of whether or not I've shared the writing project
with men I meet comes up often in my discussions about this
work. Initially, I don't tell the men anything because I don't
want them to unmatch me, call me crazy, or keep spicy pictures for blackmail. Having said that, protecting their identities is important, and I employ my skills as a researcher
of sensitive and sometimes illegal topics to make sure this
happens. My notes do not include real names or information that can easily identify anyone I've met. I haven't sani-
tized or drained the people I've encountered of their vibrant
color, but in some instances I've changed their appearance,
career, or family situation to protect their anonymity. Certain men will recognize themselves but that's because of the
unique experience we've shared, not because I expose them
in unethical ways.

My aim is not to ridicule these guys; I want to understand
them and the role they play in shaping our contemporary dating landscape and pressing issues like masculinity, sex, and
power. As my confidence in dating and my understanding

of dating apps grow, I begin to share this information with more of my dates. Several have read draft chapters and my published stories, and they often indicate that they're touched by how I express myself and weave them into the story with care. "Men have no idea how women experience these things ... They will eat it up," one of them tells me, encouragingly.

Caveats out of the way, let the last disclaimers be known: This book is not a how-to for mastering dating platforms or a guidebook for how to get ahead in dating. It is not a grand narrative that explains everything about these apps or the people on them. It's also not the only account of the darker side of dating apps, which is something that Nancy Jo Sales, Shani Silver, Alfie Bown, and others have written excellent books about. However, it is the first deep dive into swipe culture and how it holds a mirror up to modern sexuality, gender, dating, and technology using the auto-ethnographic approach.

Dating apps have brought me to my knees, and they've made me re-evaluate myself as a feminist. This life-altering experience is also forcing me to think creatively about how to keep my integrity intact while taming the spectacle of digital dating as a healing woman on a mission to engage with the world sensually. Instead of scurrying away from the apps when they're too much or blaming myself for the many problematic encounters and heartache I experience, I want to push back, and this book is my way of doing it.

I seek to transform my frustration, heartache, and joyful discoveries into a resource that may help others come through the tunnel of digital love a little less scathed. If you have ever swiped on a dating app, you'll identify with a lot of the things I share. But even if you haven't, you'll find something to relate to because our story as a society and as a species depends a great deal on dating, mating, and love. These aspects of life are being radically transformed in our age of automation and swiping technologies, which are marketed as easy, productive, and effective tools to better organize our lives.

Dating app industries loop their tendrils into our late-capitalist aspirational goals of making life easier and less hands-on. Streamline, synergize, simplify. But what these companies rely on most is our submission to the platforms themselves, and part of what I'm trying to do in these pages is to describe what it feels like to want love while also resisting the addictive pull of platforms designed to make us swipe-dependent. I think it's important to poke a few holes in the glistening narrative about how fantastic these platforms are and remind ourselves about the control we have over how we want to love and establish connections.

Sharpening our interpersonal human skills and cultivating dating courage are some of the best ways to resist the digitization of our world. Doing this can help more of us feel encouraged and empowered by our intimate experiences and who we are. Let's tell weirder, more vulnerable stories about what it's like to use these platforms and how they're impacting us. The kinds of stories that acknowledge our individual experiences and those that bind us together as humans, not cyborgs, who swipe together under the blue skies.

ONE

Selfies for Days

Swiping through endless profile pictures, I wonder about their utility as windows into who we are. How much can we ever know about someone through these selfies? As I barrel down the digital highway of lust and romance, bumping hard against the guard rails along the way, I wonder if these images have other clues I can't yet detect. Are they a mirror or a magnifying lens? Or are they mere pixels of red, yellow, and cyan?

I cringe when that guy sends a message, yet his profile remains in my roster. He tells me that I have been kinda shitty to him and that everyone is busy, which was my excuse for not meeting up the other day. It's true. I started out fresh and sexy because I thought he would be easy, easy to impress and maybe easy to play with. But it wasn't easy because although he seems sweet and I'd like to meet him, I feel stalled by things that feel somehow unnamable in this phase of the pandemic. I go radio silent, and he wants to know why.

He looks hot in the first two pictures, which is fairly easy to do in sunglasses, and in the last one he's laughing. It's cute and makes me smile every time I swipe through his pics. Why did I bail on him? The answers to my indecision are not in his photos, they are in me. I'm trying to get past the millennial bandwidth, which is his demographic, or maybe I'm trying to understand them better. Either way, they seem as foreign as another language sometimes. So too is swiping under the threat of COVID-19.

I've grown used to treating men like JPEGs instead of people. That thick skin everyone keeps telling me I'll need to survive dating apps has begun to envelope me.

I hit it off with someone older, like older than me, from the US. He's got a warm smile and is good at spicy banter. He sends me sepia-colored pictures of his father in Vietnam that make my body shiver. They seem haunted. But then he disappears when I question a few things and attempt to move beyond the basics, which is fine but also disappointing. Was I really going to fly to Nashville, as we jokingly discussed? In my experience, international love affairs are exciting but not an effective long-term romantic strategy.

Then there's the guy who is fond of sending pictures of himself in the shower. He looks super ripped and a little vulnerable, which helps me look past the grammatical errors that accompany every message. Chatting feels easy until he slips the terms "safety" and "danger" into the conversation in ways that feel weird. I try to explain my discomfort, but he doesn't understand. He calls me "crazy" and I cancel our date. He douses each text with "lol" and says I'm a "time waster" and "cold." It's infuriating and reinforces the fact that we are speaking different gendered dialects. Just another day on Tinder.

Approximately one billion selfies are taken each day. In 2013, the term selfie was added to the *Oxford English Dictionary*, where it's defined as "a photograph that one has taken of oneself, typically with a smartphone or webcam and uploaded to a social media website." June 21 is Selfie Day and if you ever wondered what it's called when someone has a compulsive need to photograph themself, it's called "selfitis." Our modern obsession with capturing every angle of our fleshly frames and showing them to one another in the game of love and everyday life could be summarized in the following way: "I selfie, therefore I am."

On dating apps, selfies are prime real estate. Given their importance, many users tweak their profile pictures multiple times to maximize their dating outcomes. When signing up to my first platform, I tweak and scroll obsessively through my phone looking for smart, sexy pictures to attract men. It's like I'm prepping for a presentation and reminds me of workplace meetings about branding ourselves as part of our collective promotion strategies.

Where's the love in that? What about the men's pictures – what are they saying about themselves amid the fish shots, blow-up pool swans, and airplanes in flight?

Stories abound about how to improve profile pictures. Services to help make dating success happen are increasingly popular, including those provided by matchmakers, dating coaches, and so on. There are also many popular culture articles that focus on making fun of users' common mistakes. I haven't always made top-drawer selections, like when I try to flex on the kid energy I observe in a lot of the men's pictures.

I upload a sweet photo of me and my nephews at the lake with the caption: "Aren't my nephews cute?" However, it keeps disappearing. Being overly determined and under-skilled in the realm of swipe culture, I email the app's support team in a bit of a panic. Yes, people email dating app support teams. They send the following reply:

> *Hello Treena,*
> *I took a look back at your photos. Unfortunately, we cannot allow a picture of a child without a top on our app. Please do feel free to upload other pictures with your children that obey our guidelines.*

Dating app selfies hardly contain the mysteries of the universe. But certain images capture fascinating clues about the people sending them that we sometimes miss in the mindless blur of swiping. What is he really saying here? Whoa, where'd that come from? OMG, I love that. Looking at the hundreds of screen shots I've saved over the years, it hits me that beyond a visual record of the different men I have encountered, these images serve another purpose.

They can be used to trace my evolution within the dating app wilderness, from babe in the woods to seasoned pro. Yeah, him, Mr. Dick Pic guy. *That's* the guy who first ghosted me. Wow, times were lean when I was talking with him. Man, I wish *he* could have turned into something more. That's the guy who told me what BBC really means!

Along with plotting my journey through this terrain, these selfies reveal fascinating and sometimes confounding insights into masculinity, sexual communication, and swipe culture. Photos from Facebook, Instagram, and WhatsApp are also featured because most digital platforms are used by men, in particular, to gain sexual access to women and sometimes financial access, in the case of swindling. I've chosen thirteen men. This is a lucky number in many cosmological and religious contexts, and it's said to be the number of blood, fertility, and lunar potency. Sexy, dripping with life and maybe death under the moon's silver glow, sounds good to me.

Selfies Overview

Bouncing into the yoga studio one night, listening to "Lady Marmalade" by Christina Aguilera, Pink, Lil' Kim, and Mya, I reveal a surprise for my instructor. I pull out my headphones and silently swipe through some men's dating profile pics with my mouth hanging open and my eyes popping. Without skipping a tree pose, Robin says, "the extremes ... oh, the humanity." Riffing on the famous phrase from the American journalist Herb Morrison, who saw the Hindenburg airship burst into flames in 1937, he nails the array of weird, disturbing, and hot pictures.

In terms of presentation, my observations reveal that roughly one-third of men on dating apps adopt an orderly and attractive approach that clearly conveys a sense of who they are and what they *currently* look like. Many of these guys include global travel pictures and are posing in identifiable cities like NYC, Dubai, and Paris. Also very popular in the more suave profiles is the vibe that I call "chill adventurer," which refers to guys who are physically active, stylish, and laid-back. Imagine a buff thirty-two-year-old guy whitewater rafting in Colorado, then enjoying a nighttime drink session with beautiful friends on the top floor of a chic hotel. In the next picture he is reading (always a good sign) in a cream-colored room that looks too boho-chic to be his, but you never know, right?

So, what about the other two-thirds? There are so many sloppy, strange, and utterly impossible-to-decipher images that narrowing it down to one or two categories is a challenge. But some common outliers include grainy childhood pictures, which may be cute but also weird because I don't want to date a little boy. There are loads of "wild guy" pictures, where the guy is holding a beer and wearing a baseball cap backwards while screaming on a beach somewhere with his bros. Men who like to dress up, not just in trick-or-treat mode, have a field day on dating apps too. Of the costume pics, however, Spiderman seems to be the most popular.

I've seen Tinder selfies that could be on Grindr, one of the most popular dating apps among LGBTQ users, especially gay and bisexual guys. There are men in wifebeaters and cowboy boots leaning coyly into the back of a truck and others showing their bodies in ways that could be a form of humiliation (e.g., wearing short shorts, being sprayed by a hose, exposing soft bellies). These men are playing with their image and their sexuality in ways that contest dominant notions of masculinity, which are commonly linked with displays of financial success, bodily fitness, luxury destination settings, and chiseled good looks. I'm here for it.

There's the ubiquitous "man holding fish" selfie, and from my review of hundreds of these images, it's usually one of the best photos because the guys are pretty much always smiling ear to ear. Interpretations of this image abound. It's been described as a display of masculinity, a show of hyper-masculinity (think a man and his truck), a reflection of their genuine love for fishing, and a proxy for the size of men's penises. It may also just be a good laugh and a chance to poke fun at dating apps, which has been suggested to me by a match or two.

Let's explore the thirteen turning-point men and what their selfies reveal about themselves, sex, gender, and my vexing travels in the land of swipe culture.

1. The Fallacy of the Dick Pic

Unexpectedly seeing a picture of a man's genitals in the palm of your hand can be startling. A case in point is the unsolicited dick pic (UDP), those brazen pictures men take of their private bits and gleefully send via text message to women who usually do not want to see them. A lot is written about these images as harmless digital rites of passage and a way to communicate sexual arousal or intent. The explicit, sometimes hilarious, resistance women continue to launch against UDPs is documented in hundreds of YouTube videos and songs, and in endless online posts.

Particularly funny is the work of Soraya Doolbaz, who capitalizes on the popularity of these images by crafting dick pics called "dictures." As featured on her website (https://dicture.com/), these are images of real penises draped with tiny clothes, wee wigs, and little props. They combine good humor with a desire to redirect male control over what counts as sexy and which body parts get press, ushering in what Doolbaz calls a "cock revolution."

Others offer a more critical appraisal of these images. In 2016 American artist Whitney Bell developed a show called "I Didn't Ask for This: A Lifetime of Dick Pics," which features 200 unsolicited dick pics she and other women have received over the years. In a *Vice* interview with Allison Stevenson, Bell distinguishes sexy pictures shared between partners from unsolicited dick pics, which she views as an expression of male aggression.

As she says, "I love a good dick. I just don't love harassment." Bell's show simultaneously pokes fun at and shames men who think it's okay to continue this knowingly unwanted behavior. Often framed as something innately digital, dick pics can be considered part of an older lineage of men using their genitals to dominate public spaces, often for the express purpose of making women uncomfortable. Gillian Frank discusses this in her brilliant 2020 article in *Jezebel* called "Pricks in Public: A Micro History." Think of men streaking across a soccer field or the flashing culture of the 1970s, beige trench coats aflutter.

As a stated technique of weeding the lame chaste women from the fiery sexual babes, the dick pic is a dismembered approach to finding or impressing someone. It's almost sad because a lot of emotional and psychological work is thrust upon the penis, which is typically featured alone in these images and in a state of craving. Who can appease the dick? The man whose dick is featured can, of course, but that's not the function of these pictures.

My experiences with unsolicited dick pics fall somewhere between funny and disturbing. I ask one guy, who I hadn't yet met, why he's sending them, and imply that they are unwanted. He makes an offhand comment about women who don't find them appealing being prudish or "lame." Despite my prudish inquiry, the unsolicited pics keep coming and over the course of one week, I receive fifteen of them. No two are the same. I'm curious about the circulation of these images and wonder if they're somehow linked with the day of the week, special occasions, or extreme randiness. When I ask, he just says, "He he he."

Beyond the obvious "I want sex" or "I love my dick" messages, UDPs also seem to be a way for this man to reveal or confirm certain aspects of his body, including the soft skin he tells me about. Imagine a window of light reflected on an alabaster smooth bottom. They can also illuminate sexual hygiene and grooming practices, like the seasonal styling of pubic hair (see, sometimes I let it grow). These images are used in discussions about preferences and fantasies, like tokens of exchange in the digital sexual economy: If I show you, you'll tell me what I want to know.

Through steamy windows of liquid crystal and plastic, he is telling me select bits of his story and trying to divine select bits of mine. However, an unsolicited dick pic can only carry a man so far. Upon meeting him, I am struck by the disconnect between the visual prowess and the flaccid reality I am greeted with in the flesh. Where'd that sexy, fun guy go? While a picture may say a thousand words, neither it nor a series of letters strung across a screen can fully stand in for the embodied interactions through which we express our humanness.

2. The Butterfly Effect

A beautiful and sometimes terrifying expression of our primal connectedness, the butterfly effect is the idea that small things can have nonlinear impacts on a complex system. The tiny flap of an insect's wing in India can cause a tornado in Idaho or a seemingly insignificant nanoparticle can turn the world upside down during a pandemic. It's an expression of chaos theory, which is what this guy introduces into my dating life. However, the experiences gained teach me some of the most important things about swiping, which I feed on while swelling from pupa to winged creature.

After getting the "here" text, I wait about four seconds before zipping downstairs to meet my date. Spying him through the back door window, I gasp with approval and know that something sexy is going to happen. He looks good, and so do I in skinny jeans that make my butt pop and a tasteful blouse that shows just enough boob. We hug awkwardly, smiles beaming from here to the moon that will guide him home a few hours later. He playfully asks, "Wow, is this a dream?"

Stardust and oxytocin surge through our veins as we kiss on the couch and then make our way to the bedroom a few minutes later. The sex is fun and so is the chitchat afterwards, when I learn that one of his uncles is also an anthropologist. "Maybe you'll meet him," he says in a message later that night, which I read over and over while clutching myself.

Slumped on a tiny chair in the Banana Republic changing rooms two days later, I wonder why he hasn't contacted me. After buying a fuchsia V-neck sweater I reach out to him and ask if my texts are annoying. Gulp. Don't you like me? Didn't we have a great time? What does this mean to you? The indeterminateness cuts into my vulnerability while I rack my dating brain to figure things out. When he refreshes his profile pictures, I cringe and realize that he's not only interested in me. I feel like an idiot for thinking that anything special might happen.

Trudging through my neighborhood that night, I listen to Leonard Cohen's "Tower of Song." He sings about voodoo dolls that don't really look like him and encourages a woman to stick pins in him because it won't hurt. Are these guys on dating apps a bunch of voodoo dolls? Visual images to conduct magic with and on and through. It feels more like hocus-pocus and digital spells gone awry. Where's the eye of newt when you need it?

On our second date, he gives me a cool poster that sparks some much-needed hopefulness. Surely, he only gives gifts to women he likes. The next day he likes a selfie I send him, and then his texts dry up. Why did you give me that poster? Why send me beautiful black and white photos of your mother as a child only to ignore me? Where did you go? I'm clueless about how to use dating apps and feel utterly broken open.

I inhabit a dim, slippery place between confidence and craving, between holding my head up and feeling not good enough. Such is the tangled path of digital intimacy. Like the monarch butterflies who migrate from Canada to his southern homeland each winter, he too coasts along warm flyways. But unlike these winged creatures who travel long distances to propagate and pass on their genetic material, the only thing he passes on is bittersweet memories of cuteness and cowardice.

From this painful encounter, I learn that everyone is talking to a million people at once and that low expectations may be the best medicine, two valuable lessons that help see me through the years of fun and disappointment that follow.

3. Over and Out, Good Buddy

Long-haul truck drivers are among the oldest cohorts in the Canadian work force and are, on average, around fifty years old. I learn this while doing a Google search during a fifteen-minute conversation with a long-distance truck driver who is a mere thirty-one years old. As we talk, I wonder if he knows "Convoy" by C.W. McCall. This hilarious song features several unforgettable characters named Rubber Duck, Pig Pen, and Spider Mike, along with a host of other truck drivers who band together against corrupt state troopers. The 1978 film of the same name stars Kris Kristofferson and Ali MacGraw and had a catchy tag line: "Ain't nothing gonna get in their way." It was part of a short-lived but righteous pop culture trend of celebrating the outlaw truck driver making his way across the USA.

I send him an image of the *Convoy* movie poster and turns out he knows the movie. I also learn that he loves cats and just bought a female Persian feline (men often have female cats, I find), who he intends on taking to work. This situation is, of course, a 2.0 version of *B.J. and the Bear*, the late 1970s/early 1980s television series about an itinerant truck driver and his trusty chimpanzee named Bear.

Research demonstrates that we tend to select mates based on how similar they are to us, but experience has shown me that having a few differences also stokes the fires of love, lust, or even just a good conversation. That's what transpired between me and this young trucker – a truly random and enjoyable chitchat about small chunks of our life on a Saturday afternoon. There are no formulaic questions about sex or mention of a date, and the unforced nature of our exchange stands out as unique.

After we say goodbye, I scroll through his photos again to see if I can get a more in-depth read on him. This turns out to be kind of hard because his selfies are super scattered and bring to mind the song "The Real Slim Shady." Who is this guy, anyways?

In the lead image he looks sun-kissed and smiles next to a woman who's been messily scratched out. Why not just crop her out, bro? He's rocking an unfortunate hairstyle that's reminiscent of Jim Carrey in *Dumb and Dumber*. It's weird but, then again, it's a classic movie so I'm willing to let it go. In the next picture he's wearing a red wig and looks super hot – built, tall, sexy. In the last one he's standing next to a red sports car that's parked near a dodgy-looking apartment building, the kind that you might drive by just before entering an industrial park.

I zoom in on his face and see traces of a thin mustache. A pang of regret sets in for his being so nice and fun in our chat. This visceral reaction takes me by surprise and is soon replaced by feelings of "Hey, whatever, a guy who likes cats, that's awesome." Does it really matter if he has a small mustache and is a bit country? It might, but then again ours is a meeting that moves underneath the screen and ain't nothing gonna get in our way because there ain't nothing happening beyond a fun swipe and chat. Toot-toot.

4. Koi Boi

The word "koi" comes from the Japanese term for carp. In Japan, koi symbolize love and friendship, along with luck, good fortune, and perseverance in the face of adversity. These colorful ornamental fish have been bred in Japan and other parts of Asia since the eighth century, and they swim along the arms of men who decorate themselves in ink. One such man swooshes into my palm, which begins to pulse when I set eyes on his bulgy biceps and meaty forearms covered in a tapestry of marine-inspired reds, blues, greens, and yellows.

He wears a basic white t-shirt, has short well-styled brown hair, and has strong-looking hands that grip his white iPhone. He stands in the bathroom mirror and raises his right eyebrow in that way that says, "I'm hot and you might have a chance." I can't let this one go, I say to myself while scrambling for something hot to text. His profile says "fun and friendship," which is code for casual sex, and so I send this: "Hey beautiful, we should get together."

My shoulders scrunch up in delight when he replies to me seconds later: "You're gorgeous." OMG, this might work, this could turn into something cool. With my loin-driven imagination fired up, we have a few back and forths about sexual interests. He baits me by saying, "You're probably too nice for me ..." – a statement designed to cultivate a bad boy image and make me reveal the naughty things I've done to see if I can match his repertoire.

A lot of men, especially younger ones, use this approach, which I find a bit boring but play along for the sake – or is it saké? – of the potential prize.

As the #2 bus pulls into the university campus bus stand, I hop on and eagerly return to my dating conversation. But koi boi has vanished. My stomach turns in frantic knots and my face goes crimson. What happened? I email Bumble customer service and explain what took place, while checking my roster repeatedly. Baby's first ghosting.

What makes this example so wild is that this guy does the same thing four more times within the span of a month. I keep swiping right on him because, somewhere in my lonely dark corner, I hope something might happen. Plus, he is so hot, like so hot. After the third ghosting, I ask him why he's behaving like this, and he says, "Bad timing ... Still sort of in something with my ex." I'm calling your bluff, you ornamental gigolo. Didn't you like me? That's how we matched, isn't it?

These heart-grinding questions are scattered throughout my early dating app days when I'm working so hard to understand why people ghost. I don't have a lot of answers other than they can and that using digital platforms to communicate dulls our ability to cultivate empathy and compassion. When people are perceived of as pixels, they don't really exist and that enables us to swipe mindlessly and with ferocity, sometimes hundreds of times per day on multiple apps.

We'd never say "no," "NO," "nope," or "nooo" to the faces of two hundred people lined up in a hallway or standing on a grassy hillside. We don't do it because it's mean.

A lot is written about ghosting because it's so common and because it feels so terrible. The new app Tame bans ghosting, and if you ghost someone on Bumble you could be banned. Although it's not clear how well these new apps and policies will work, they're an important step in taking this awful practice more seriously than is usually the case. Being ghosted robs of us of the sensory responses we need to communicate with the people we're dating or talking to. I can't start crying or yell at koi boi because he's not there to see or hear me. I can't even send angry texts because he literally no longer exists. Where do I put my bubbling anger and vicious feelings of being ugly, fat, and a failure in love? They get stored inside my body, in a little box called "warning: this may happen again."

5. Let's Pretend This Never Happened

Catfish is the name of an American documentary that debuted at the Sundance Film Festival in 2010. It explores the experiences of a guy who travels from New York City to Gladstone, Michigan, to connect with a nineteen-year-old woman he met on Facebook. However, when they meet, he discovers that she's really a forty-year-old housewife with addiction issues and that multiple family members were involved in the deceptive communication.

At one point, the woman's stepfather relays a story about catfish and codfish, who are natural enemies. Catfish are often shipped in the same tanks as codfish to keep them active, a technique used to maintain the quality of the fish. The stepfather likens this process to that of the catfish in his family, who seems to like keeping other people alert. That's one way to put it.

Catfishers on dating apps usually pretend to be someone they're not for financial reasons or to avoid rejection because of their appearance. Women tend to catfish more often than men, but I've encountered a few ballsy bottom-feeders. There's something about catfish pictures that sets off my spidey sense. It's not just that the guys are over-the-top hot, it's the images themselves. Instead of personalized selfies, they look like cardboard stock photos of pretty guys who could be eating sushi or working out anywhere on the planet.

Take the case of the guy who swam into my shipping box, twice.

The first time it happens I recall thinking that his three profile pictures almost match. Almost? Two of them are definitely the same guy, but the third one looks a bit different. I tell myself that I don't mind who shows up because they both look juicy! None of the men featured in the profile pictures arrive at my apartment, and the one that does looks nothing like anyone in the photos. I didn't get the memo in the dating app manual that explains what I'm supposed to do when faced with a catfish. I'm shocked but have to hide it, for fear of being seen as rude, and I'm pretty sure these fish bank on our silence.

What am I going to say? "Excuse me, you're not what was advertised." I say neither and sleep with him because I'm interested in sex and because it seems potentially dangerous to turn down this stranger, who's very well-built and looks strong. If you're wondering why I invite him to my apartment, it's because at this point in my sobriety meeting at a bar makes me uncomfortable. I feel safe in my small apartment building, where my neighbors are home at all hours. I'm not advocating this approach to others, just being honest about how events unfolded. In this instance, the sex was pretty fun. However, when he begins asking me for money, I delete him and move on.

Fast-forward to a pandemic Friday night a couple years later when I'm back on Tinder after a relationship-induced hiatus. I'm stoked to have a date with this hottie who's also a responsive communicator. But his profile pics don't look entirely consistent. I let it slide because, hey, it's been a while. When I spy him coming out of the cab, I feel my insides drop. He's not as tall as any of the men in his pics, and when he removes his face mask a series of small red flags begin pushing their way through my intuitive landscape.

I show him to the living room and a voice inside me says, "I know this man, it's the same guy from before."

He asks me questions and casually unpacks a half empty plastic bottle of vodka and then a container of cranberry juice from inside his bag. He's brought his own glass too. When he tosses his cardigan onto the chair next to him, I see the large arm tattoo. Bingo. A few seconds later, I say, "I think we've met before," and he says no, stone-faced, while adding that he was seeing someone two years ago. Then he asks for details of my interactions with this guy (HIM) and I say there's not much to recall. Then I mention that we slept together and still nothing.

He says repeatedly that we haven't met and drops this racially provocative comment: "Are you saying all Black guys look the same?" Further fueling the gaslighting shitshow, he adds that it would be messed up for someone to do that. Yes, sir, you are correct. Bizarrely, he also says this: "If we did meet, it must have been in another time." Another time? What a time-traveling fraud! I say that I'm not feeling it and he slowly packs up his vagabond booze while calling a cab.

When I escort him to the door he whispers, "Let's pretend this never happened," which makes me break out in a cold sweat. I want to scream "CATFISHER" but don't feel safe and, sadly, I have no recourse to report him because he unmatched me before getting into the taxi. What would Tinder do with three fake pictures, anyway?

6. Amateur Aperture

When we move between bright and dark environments, the iris expands or shrinks to control our pupil size and the amount of light we see. Remember turning the dimmer left and right, or the switch up and down, while watching this happen in the mirror? The aperture on a camera, sometimes called "the pupil," works in a similar way by shrinking and enlarging as the photographer chooses to allow more or less light to reach the camera sensor. A book by the provocative American photographer Diane Arbus is also called *Aperture*, and it was published posthumously in 1971, a year before I was born.

Like the arresting images Arbus is known for, including dead ringer sets of twins and tender renderings of socialites and circus performers alike, this man's lead selfie is etched in my mind. He looks to his left through tinted aviators and his right dark-jeaned leg is in mid-stride as he descends the stairs of what looks like a private plane. Gently gripping the stair rails, I see a pop of neon green on his left wrist, a tasteful and original timepiece. Drool. The bottom of his crisp white shirt flutters under a black blazer that fits to a titillating T and shows the arch of his muscular frame.

Part Taye Diggs and Seal, he is all the things my wet dreams are made of and when those magic yellow words splash across my screen – It's a Match! – I squeal in astonishment.

It's around 7:30 a.m. and, besides his scrumptious appearance and interesting profession as a photographer, I like that this man begins his day early. When he asks to switch from the app to regular texting I gleefully agree and send him a message right away. When he responds with "Who is this?" I feel a wave of panic crash over me. OMG, how embarrassing. "Sorry! Yes, it's Treena," I reply, to which he says: "I thought so, but wanted to make sure."

A phrase I see tossed around this bee-inspired platform begins to sink in: "Bumble to stay humble." Point aptly made; I hungrily wait for his next cue. He offers up an easy morsel and asks about my job, which intrigues more than a few "sapiosexuals" out there, referring to people who say they're turned on by intelligence.

Trying desperately to seem cool, I inquire about being a photographer and non-casually mention Diane Arbus. He seems impressed and talk quickly turns to making a date for the coming weekend. He's in Toronto, where I just happen to be going for the weekend. The energies of the universe are aligning and a date with this superstar will be the cherry on my CN Tower, which is located about 190 kilometers away.

By the time I make it to my window seat on the Saturday morning train, I'm humming with erotic anticipation. What will it feel like to be next to someone so beautiful? Are my shirt dress and cool shoes okay or will he mistake me for a peasant? How long will we spend together?

We are meeting at 2 p.m. and my mind drifts to what we might talk about and what we might do. Then I get a text from Taye/Seal, confirming that we're on for this afternoon. "YES, can't wait!" I reply. His next message is a little off-putting because he asks where I live, which is written in my profile. When I say "London," he pauses and tells me that long-distance dating isn't something he does but it's okay because I'm coming into town anyway. I let out an exasperated sigh and resume my fantasizing.

But then the aperture closes and my stomach coils when I read the next text he sends me, twenty minutes later: "Yeah, I'm going to cancel our date. I'm meeting someone local at 2 p.m. instead." This train I'm on is really a roller-coaster and reminds me of some things I will never forget: (1) Toronto men don't leave downtown; (2) People don't read the profiles; and (3) Diane Arbus was right when she said, "It's important to take bad pictures. It's the bad ones that have to do with what you've never done before. They can make you recognize something you hadn't seen in a way that will make you recognize it when you see it again" (Arbus 1971, 10).

7. Gross like Sunday Morning

Limerence is a state of mind resulting from obsessive thoughts, fantasies, and/or a desire to maintain a relationship with people we love. It also includes wanting to have our feelings reciprocated. This evocative term was coined by American psychologist Dorothy Tennov in her 1977 book *Love and Limerence: The Experience of Being in Love* and it sums up some of the feelings I have while swiping on dating apps.

Alas, these limerick-sounding emotions were nowhere to be found the Sunday morning I sent a cute opening line to the preppy imposter.

His super clean-cut vibe isn't really my go-to, but a sharp-dressed guy with unique style gets top starter points in my dating almanac. His son, who is featured in most of his selfies, seems to share his dad's love for checked button-up shirts and bow ties. They both wear glasses and look pleased as punch to be together. Plus, he's on Bumble, which is several rungs up from the pedestrian hookups other apps are known for; he must be okay! While composing my message, I let my fingers take their time.

The distance between us is fairly significant and the likelihood of us actually getting together is pretty low. Still, I compliment his look, make an observant note about his profession, and press send with a smile.

Processing his abrupt hypersexualized response takes more than a few seconds. I clutch my chest while marveling at the speed and precision of his replies. It's like he's just waiting, his small hands floating deviously above the tiny keyboard on his phone. He spews a bunch of incel fantasies that are so repelling that I almost laugh out loud. It's 9:30 a.m. on a Sunday, where do you get the balls to talk to me like this?

ME: ... WOW
HIM: Show me pics of your pussy? 🐱
Lol
ME: ... yeah ...
HIM: TMI
ME: Kinda. I guess sex underlies a lot of what happens here
     and I'm desiring that too ... just seemed a little harsh
HIM: I'm naked and hard
Just love it

The pics of my pussy he refers to are the cats that I mention in my opening line. But I'm sufficiently grossed out by his descriptions of what he wants to do to me that I'm at a loss for words – no pussy shot for you. I say that he's acting kind of harsh and seems pretty focused on himself, which only inspires more repugnant musings. He claims to be selfless in bed and provides additional descriptions of the hot sex he will lay out and how much and loud I will orgasm in response. I want to barf.

Then, a photo is sent. I open the image and am greeted by a modest chest dotted with an assortment of brown moles. It is richly covered in dark hair and set against a stark white trunk. Two small legs jut out on either side of the body and between them sits a small member, which reaches up and over to the left. A nugget of bile begins its dark upwards climb from my gut to my throat as he keeps sending messages.

I don't respond and just watch this gross horror unfold in the palm of my hand. I swallow hard to keep the vomit at bay and delete this preppy-gone-bad with no limerence in sight.

The shock and whir of this exchange is sort of funny, but it's also awful. It makes me think about the infinite layers of patriarchy's web and what it feels like to be caught in its sticky membrane. It's an unwanted place that, as a woman, I am destined to rub up against my whole life. We're not safe in our homes or in the streets, what about in our own bodies as we scroll for the love and lust we deserve? Nope, not there either. Who's at the center of this web?

I imagine a little boy wearing old-timey cloth shorts and a button-up shirt, leather shoes, and socks that come just past the ankles. A flock of freckles scatter across his milky face, and he's got red hair and maybe a cowlick or two. He is the scamp, the truant boy, the cheeky brat who's plastered across postwar advertisements for everything from orange juice to ADHD medication. I wish I could banish the web as easily as I delete the impish dad.

8. Swindler Selfie

Most of us use multiple online platforms for networking, getting directions, and connecting with friends. Folks looking for romance move between these digital spaces too, which can overlap in weird ways that include getting what I call "Hi'd" by men whose modus operandi mirrors the deceptive tactics of dating app swindlers. I've typed "UMMM, I don't use this platform for dating, and I don't even know you" endless times in my Facebook and Instagram accounts. Like pesky weeds, these messages pop up in my social media inbox more frequently.

A case in point is this DM I recently received, copied here verbatim. Verbatim? Yes, I copy it here word for word because it's so stupid, false, and frankly doesn't even make sense.

> Hello beautiful my name is Harrison Greg I'm 60years born in Sweden to a natives of US my dad is from Alabama while my mother is from Ohio ,I'm a marine engineer currently working with Maersk oil I'm currently on a vessel in the north sea somewhere close to the UK, I'm sorry to invade your privacy, I couldn't pass without saying hi your just too beautiful your profile fits perfectly to my kind of woman, your beauty is like the heavens. I'm on here trying to make a new friend that could possibly lead to something beautiful am looking forward to hearing from you

Every swindler selfie who bombards me with messages does not use my actual name and begins with a dramatic set of events designed to pull me in. In this instance, a hard-working, well-paid man adrift in the middle of the ocean looking for some TLC. What's not to jump at? "Harrison" even apologizes for invading my privacy, what a gentleman. The apology is what gets me because it's like he, or the bot behind this masquerade, thinks that by issuing it I'll forget that he is violating my privacy. Not likely.

Then there's the surgeon named "Henderson" – do they get these names from the same digital hat? – who contacts me on Tinder and then WhatsApp. He wears cute scrubs that look like they've never been used and drops phrases like "my dear" and "love" out of the gate. Then he sends a weird poem about me being "God's design ... the best woman." This might be true, but *who* are you again? Infuriated and semi-intrigued, I call his number and am shocked that he picks up. His voice sounds squeaky, and he giggles after telling me I'm "sooo hottt" and he's getting a boner.

The man in his profile selfie looks confident, calm, and sexy, but the one on the phone sounds like a pubescent derp. When I press him to tell me what his deal is, he says, "Whatever you like. Your wish is my command." OMG, open sesame – who is this love bomb genie?

Sometimes they're single Christian dads, with seven or eight squeaky-clean outdoor images that are all posted on the same day. Many are American, in the military, or hold dual citizenship, as reflected in the national flag emojis featured in their profiles. Almost all of these Instagram or Facebook accounts are private, which gives the gloss of exclusivity and security, but I can't see anything beyond their lead photo and bios.

Why would I follow back or add as a friend? How many women do? Enough, it seems, to make this premeditated strategy of digital invasion a universal phenomenon.

I use various strategies to cope with this slime of aggressive male attention, including telling the men to stop. I block them and post their stupid replies on social media in frustration. I sometimes ask them why they engage in this random dating strategy. They all respond in exactly the same way, by professing ignorance to any problematic behavior on their part, saying that we can develop something beautiful together, and asking me to give them a chance.

It's chilling when my expression of "no" has its meaning so carved out that it's nothing more than a hollow space made by two letters. I am in those spaces, as a woman. If not no, what can I say? What is my vocabulary of protection or prevention? Is there a way to make men and the companies creating the coercive bots listen?

These invasions aren't about dating, they're manifestations of the digital patriarchal creep. They're also not random or ridiculous, as men's behavior, online and otherwise, is often described. A recent *Cosmo* article indicates that love bombing is often unconscious and can be considered a kind of personality disorder. Such a perspective is not helpful because it reduces this misogynistic behavior to the actions of a few "bad apples" and reducing it to a medical condition decontextualizes it from the broader culture of gender-based violence that informs this digital aggression. Swindler, go home!

9. Talking to a Tree

1 Profile – John, 33
      Looking for FWB
      I don't judge you. you don't judge me.
      I'm not anyone's cup of tea.
      Neither will you be.
      Pics, you'll get to see.
      Yes I'm 33.
      You must like the D.
      Or stay away from me.

2 Profile – J, 33
      FWB
      No flat asses
      No time wasters
      No psychos
      No baggage
3 J, 33
      Looking for one fwb. No one nighters!

The NSFW (not safe or suitable for work) tree photo that accompanies these profiles is famous online and Tommy Lee, yes, that Tommy Lee, has posted it on his Instagram. I see it repeatedly on more than one dating app and discern that it's one guy doing it. I mean how many people would choose the "trees fucking" picture repeatedly? Although the profile information varies somewhat, he's always called "J" or something like it. Each time this image pops up in my feed I wonder who this is and why he's using this picture. So, I match with him and ask him about it:

ME: Hi there, I have to ask about this photo. I see it often on here. What's it about?

J: Hi, it's just a tree, but if you look closer, it looks like a man behind a woman doing doggy lol.

ME: I got that, I just find it odd I guess!!

J: You man the fact that you've seen it often? It could be just me making another account because I ran out of people to swipe on! Mean*

ME: I've seen different men use it, that's weird. I guess I think it's weird to use pictures of trees VS. who you are too. You ran out of people!!???

J: Not allowed to put a sexual pic on here, this one is not
banned. I don't post my own pic because I work with 300
employees some I've seen on Tinder, I'd rather not show
myself due to the nature of what I'm seeking.

ME: Ah, I see.

J: I know you were just curious, but are you interested in anything else?

ME: What do you mean? Talking with a tree feels a bit silly,
tbh. It seems to add an extra layer in what's already kinda
ridiculous. Have you met up with a lot of women on here?
The pandemic seems to have made people's behavior so
weird.

10. Pandemic Holding Pattern

When an airplane's designated path is suspended, it does
laps in the sky waiting for clearance in what's called a
holding pattern. Scrambling around mid-air and wanting
nothing more than to walk on solid ground captures the
grim reality of dating in the early vaccine times. People
swipe on dating apps in record numbers, but in-person
dates and sex don't come roaring back as many researchers predict.

Most of the time it's like we're looking at one another from
inside our hungry skin, suspended somewhere far above
the desires we crave. Although the offerings are meager,
my thrill-spot never stops flickering and I'm determined to
date.

On my way to the coffee shop, I pass used car lots and
electronic shops closed for the night. The sun begins its yolky
descent and the breeze blowing through my hair makes me

feel sexy. But then I notice him loitering near a gray minivan and my mojo flees. I almost pretend not to see him because he's so not my type. But my types aren't responding and perhaps going through the motions of romance will fill some of the aching spaces inside me. I put on a quick smile when we say "hello" and put one foot in front of the other. I can do this.

During the stilted first few minutes of our conversation, I study the thin sheaves of brown hair on his forearms and can't get over how clean the empty café is. Then my date asks, "So, have you always had this Zen calmness that radiates in such an obvious way?" This observant query stops me in my unenthralled tracks. So, instead of rolling my eyes when he wants to know about my tattoos, which number around seventy and counting, I share some of the colorful stories behind the ink on my body.

When he whips up the sleeves of his shirt to reveal two pieces of his own, which are fairly rudimentary in design but legit, I'm impressed. With kids, marriages, and an orthodox religious background, his path couldn't be more different than mine.

Things wrap up around 8 p.m. and we chat for a few minutes next to his Dodge Caravan before saying goodbye. I sense that we're both relieved that tonight was fun. When I suggest getting together again, he nods and says, "yes, please don't ghost me!" We laugh and I walk home along the quiet, run-down streets between the cafe and my place.

The odd person peeps out of a dusky window, and I think about this guy's caring but lonely face, the one who saw me for the first time in forever. This recognition glows like a shard in my pocket, illuminating my thoughts. Could I kiss him? Do I want him to explore me?

The second date starts strong but then morphs into a drawn-out game of "who did more crazy stuff in their twenties." As he talks, I glance at his hands. Although large, they look like computer hands, not the kind that can easily toss me around and make me slick. Despite the scream of every ancient cell in my amygdala that says "don't do it," I ask if he wants to get together again. Stoke that soggy fire, girl.

While munching on home fries with him a few days later, I learn that he's planning a celestial tattoo with his children as the planets. But he only has four kids, not eight, and I hear myself question the design in a snappy tone. The bitch in me is rising to the surface because I'm prolonging what I know is doomed and because this guy is what's available at the moment.

I don't remember anything else we talk about and when he pauses at the door for a kiss, I smile and bounce awkwardly back into my house. Because men find me attractive, I often think that they want to spend time with me, and this misplaced assumption can make me careless in the way I treat them. It's selfish to drag someone who I have no romantic interest in into my furious, sad drama. He knows it too.

The next day he tells me he's going to pursue something with someone else, adding that I'm a "solid person but hard to read." I respect this but also feel a little #meangirl miffed that *he* dumped *me*. A selfie arrives from this guy a few days later that features a mind-bending depiction of the cosmos on his chest. It has a crooked feeling, like those twelfth-century Byzantine paintings where the Christ Child looks like a wizened old man and the castles are really out of perspective. I won't say it feels like karma, but I will say that it reminds me of the importance of trying to be kinder to some men and reading the universe inside myself more carefully.

11. Tattoo Treachery

The word treachery is synonymous with treason, which conjures up images of mangy-haired pirates with jigsaw teeth who wear burlap clothes while fiendishly cavorting on wooden vessels and stealing booty from the crown. It also denotes feelings of deep and unforgivable betrayal, which makes sense because the term originated from the twelfth-century French words *trecherie* and *tricherie*, which mean "deceit, cheating, trickery, and lies."

Into my digital viewfinder pounces a modern marauder, and like his wayward ancestors who were marked with state-sanctioned tattoos announcing their criminality, he too is filled with black ink. Tribal designs cascade across his muscular body, and the large, rounded curves and points seem like strategically designed beacons of badness and sexiness. Ahoy, Matey. Thirty-two years old and named after a cool southern American city, he's an early Thanksgiving treat that I'm eager to gobble.

Faint bleeps on my intuitive sonar begin the moment we match. This guy is too good-looking. These subtle warnings continue while I study his selfies in as much detail as the zoom function on my phone allows and wait to see if he messages me. I'm hot, I can get guys like this, I hear myself saying, with slight trepidation.

He says "hi gorgeous," which feels good no matter what the creep meter says. It encourages me to try to make this work because he's into me, which is what I want. The floating dots inside the rectangle of his incoming reply indicate that he's typing, but they move agonizingly slow. I provide my digits to keep things moving. After the basic questions about what we each "do" for work and our respective "Tinder goals" (i.e., casual, see what happens), he begins the "have you ever?" questions designed to gauge my sexual repertoire and flaunt his carnal sophistication.

Insert rolling-eye emoji. Men usually ask the same things and the responses, although marginally interesting, have very little bearing on what actually transpires in the flesh. Yes, I've had sex in public and, yes, I've let someone kiss my ass, now can we arrange an in-person meeting? No scheduling information is provided, and he continues sexual steamrolling, using polite language like, "If I may ask ..." He then wants to show me his "BIG" cock in exchange for pictures of me.

Although I don't want to, I quickly take a couple of basic, not-too-revealing shots to increase my chances of meeting this sailorly stud. What I receive next is a very close up image of a massive soft cock falling out of the zipper of a pair of jeans. I see red bumpy shave marks at the base of the shaft, which makes me cringe. That must hurt.

He then pulls me into a sinister game of guess the cock size, which I must do in three tries or send him a pussy shot. Hiss, hard hiss. I'm so stupid for sending this guy nice pictures of myself and for getting fooled by yet another digital charlatan. I tell him no pussy shots and that he'll just have to wait for our in-person rendezvous. Alive with nervous energy and feeling very tangled up in his coercive game, I want to out his swashbucklingness but don't know how.

It's seemingly impossible to know when anyone on dating apps is being honest and if any of them give a shit about how they make me feel. I ask where he lives and when he's coming to see me, and he says a place that roughly jives with the 133 kilometers between us and that a visit could happen in a "month-ish … if that works for you."

When I ask why so long, he says, "Busy with work and shit, it sucks." I'm sorry, you told me that you're a private chef and that you play pool for a living. That's a strenuous schedule, hey? I leave a voicemail about how creepy and boring this is, to which he replies: "wat u sent didn't work." WAT = a voicemail, check it out. So, I type what I said and he's like "Ok got so u think I'm boring. Ok no prob if you ain't interested that's fine."

No, not you, but those questions and your tone totally shifted, which makes me super uncomfortable. I mention a phone call to talk this out and he sends me the following text instead, which is devoid of all punctuation: "Well if u don't feel comfy then may you don't want to which is fine also up to u." Gas, meet light.

12. The Guy Who's Always There

There is a man whose selfie surfaces every time I reopen a dating app account or try my luck on a new platform. He looks eerily the same in all of his selfies, which never include a body shot. Is there something untoward about his body? His head and neck look a little elongated, maybe he's tall, too tall. But then again, height is one of the biggest determinants of dating success for men so perhaps that's not the issue.

He is always in the "already swiped right on me" category but I don't reciprocate. He doesn't look attractive or interesting, although I'd be lying if I said I didn't almost swipe right on his photo during some lean times in the pandemic. I also consider matching with him to learn about who he is in order to fill in the blanks of the story I've been weaving on my digital loom for years.

Seeing him strikes something in me each time. Am I also going to be on here for years looking for someone? Hasn't he had any luck? He is like a timestamp in my dating app odyssey, marking and reminding me of what I have learned, done, and, sometimes, what I want to forget about this complex experience. What does he think when he sees me?

13. The Man in the Garden

There are moments when you both reach for the apple at the same time, and this is one of them. He gardens and knows the earth. In his lead selfie he looks like a Viking deity. He has sun-kissed blond hair blowing away from his angular face, and his green eyes glow with the fire of something deep. "Kind and wise" is how a friend described his look, which makes me feel like I'm in good company. That's how I am, too.

Beyond the adventuresome, athletic, fun man in the selfies, I learn of the self-doubt and hurt that ripple through his lithe body. Love lays like a hidden swell in his four chambers, protected by the muscle of memory. Beyond this, I rely on words written three weeks after we met. When my heart was already wet and open.

Gasps tumble from your mouth and echo through the bedroom as my tongue traces the long meat of your neck. On the grey patterned sheets, below the Escher wallpaper, the hands of time vanish as we enter and re-enter each other in the darkness.

"Open or closed?" you ask as things begin to smolder, referring to the drapes. The question excites me because it reveals an adventure-someness and a willingness, a desire perhaps, to be seen.

I nestle myself in your brulee skin and soft hair as the afternoon becomes night. Each rhythmic wave you make of your body finds its way inside mine. You look like a golden swan, so beautifully sup-ple. Your groin, your strong fingers, and your sweaty chest become smeared with my scent.

Me. I am planting myself in you, a man of soil, plants, and travel. We're growing something that feels wild and about time.

When you tuck yourself into me, I feel the years that have not been gentle to you. The women who haven't touched you like I do. I keep caressing you to tell you how beautiful you are. How much you deserve the attention you give others. How much I like you.

The wetter I get the louder you get, joyous in my slippery juices. You say my pussy feels like velvet and tastes good. All I can say is "ooh fuuckk" and "Ohh my Goood."

I must have uttered these things a hundred times as we pant in unison, and you hit my spot over and over. My come and our spit and hair slither around me and up my back. I pick you and me out of my mouth and grin like a maniac in the pitch-dark room.

Selfie Stories, So What?

Dating apps are a fast game of luck that lure you in with promises of easy, fun connection. It all happens in the blink of a swipe. But what determines if our thumbs go left or right? The written blurbs are important, but it's really the selfies that keep things moving. Is this mindless objectification? Many aspects of swipe culture are approached in a mindless way because they're routinized and we're encouraged, as good little dating app consumers, to be constantly swiping our hearts out. Although reducing one another to JPEGs is normalized in modern romance, these acts and the images that determine our dating journeys are far from meaningless.

Beneath the screen and between the bodies that swipe there is a universe to explore. There's our personal fears, lusts, and desires for intimacy as well as the deception that can impact whose pictures we swipe on, which direction we move them, and how we make sense of these experiences. The thirteen selfies in this chapter represent turning points in my sojourn through swipe culture. What do they reveal about issues like masculinity, sexual communication, and the swipe culture that informs how we use dating apps?

Masculinity
mas·cu·lin·i·ty
/maskyə'linədē/

noun
1 qualities or attributes regarded as characteristic of men.
   "handsome, muscled, and driven, he's a prime example of masculinity"

Robust physical characteristics and socio-economic drive have traditionally defined our ideas of what it means to be a successful heterosexual man. Sometimes called "industrial masculinity" because of its links with the industries of mass production, factories, and farming, this model of manhood is being joined by other options that reflect our shifting cultural world. Bring on the men in skirts, the ripped guys at the gym, man buns, and the straight men who love pegging – it's all part of the stew of modern masculinity. These shifts are reflected on dating platforms.

Do I go for the guy whose lead selfie features him pulling on a packed bong while his polyamorous partner peeks over his shoulder? How about the softer-looking guy in the cool shirt with a cat on his shoulder? No, but I respect the fact that men are showing more of themselves in their profiles.

Although I often tell people that I don't have a "type," that might not be entirely accurate. In fact, I may be guilty of being primarily attracted to the old-school industrial types – viva la assembly line. Almost all of the men featured in this chapter are good-looking, physically fit, and their selfies reflect a sense of adventure, good style, and travel savvy. This is how I see myself; like attracting like, I suppose.

Not that I think I'm gorgeous, but if I'm working hard to be the best me in my job, my look, and overall life, and that's what I want in the men I meet. Being with someone who's super nice but not the other things is something that never works in my high-stakes, sometimes pretentious Sagittarius realm. To thine own self be … true.

Dating practices like making the first move, leading the conversation, and suggesting when and where to meet have typically been considered the domain of men. However, within the realm of swipe culture these activities are being transformed, and with the exception of Bumble, where women always make the first move, I undertake these behaviors as often as the men I swipe on do. Many of my matches say that they appreciate when I take the lead in reaching out and suggesting date ideas, which signals their desire to share this dating labor.

But I also encounter men who poke fun at my upfront, sex-positive communication style. The first time one of these incel types says I'm behaving "like a man," I almost shit a psychedelic disco brick. Um, the 1970s called and they want their retrograde terminology back.

The most compelling observation about masculinity on dating platforms is that it's in flux, not just in terms of doing manhood but also in terms of how men relate to women. In the post-#MeToo era, in particular, a lot is being revealed regarding how much sexism, gender inequity, and violence women have to deal with and how uncomfortable some men are when the scales of power tip a little in our favor.

As discussed in many of the selfie stories, misogyny streams through dating apps and is reflected in the images, language, and sexual expectations as well as desires expressed by many matches. At times, this makes me feel sad, angry, and very hopeless about romance and men.

Our societal system breeds deep-rooted fears of women and anyone who wants to live outside of the boxes we are assigned. It also destabilizes men who are curious about different ways of being themselves, as well as what women are really like, and are worried about having an indeterminate place in the changing world. Patriarchy deserts them and asks for loyalty at the same time. No thank you.

There is considerable vulnerability among men, along with their urge to connect, which I learn over and over again. But these feelings are often masked by darker behaviors that reflect the complexities of love, sex, and relating to one another in our male-dominated society.

Sexual Communication

Sexualized communication between myself and the thirteen men takes many forms. The body is front and center, beginning with the dick. Sometimes a dick pic is just a dick pic. But the unsolicited dick pic is a cultural symbol of male power that's used to target women and ridicule us when we recoil from these images. This was seen in the first selfie story, when the guy in question implies that women who don't like dick pics are lame. Why did he want to reduce himself – so often – to his genitals, though? Did he think his dick is better looking than his face?

For this guy, who turns out to be a super-nervous introvert, talking about himself and his desires through images that contain a lot of built-in meanings associated with male sexual power may be easier than engaging in successful in-person dialogue with an attractive woman. I'll never really know because after our tragic in-person date, communication between us evaporated.

The dick is also used by the preppy dad, who sends me that awful picture of his feeble chest and unnoteworthy genitals. His violent texts, which never stop despite my lack of reply and expression of discomfort, are used alongside the selfies in a show of male sexual aggression. The tattoo treachery dude also ignores me when I say I don't send pussy shots and then tries to rope me into a gag-worthy game of guess his cock size. If that even is his cock. I feel like a hole, like something they want to fill with their digital spunk, anger, and weakened power.

When such harmful practices occur on a global scale, and on platforms other than dating apps (remember the swindler selfie), they're solidified as normal. Framing them as funny and harmless makes them harder to question and categorize as misogynistic. This is why I rarely say anything about getting unwanted dick pics. There are so many things in these exchanges that I don't like; I have to decide what to voice my opposition to and what to ignore. An image of skin and muscle is less threatening than when men's tone changes from polite to aggressive, or when they try to gaslight me.

Thankfully, men on dating apps communicate their sexual experiences and fantasies in nonviolent ways as well. Many of them are playful and don't even mention sex in our initial conversations, including *Convoy* boy, the photographer who dumps me on the train, the crooked cosmos tattoo guy, the guy who's always there, and the god in the garden. The talking tree is a special case in many ways, and although he speaks about using that image in lieu of a more sexual picture, he's polite and seemingly engaged in our conversation about his unique selfie.

Swipe Culture

One of the most compelling things these selfie stories illuminate about swipe culture is that using dating apps is something that is learned. In anthropological lingo, this is called "enculturation," which refers to the process of learning about one's own culture. For digital natives, mastering these platforms might be basic, but for this Gen X maiden it's a bewildering terrain that I wander through, very lost, for longer than I care to admit. Is it even dating? When did surveillance and sexting take the place of a good romp and the sound of a new lover's voice?

The selfie stories reflect many negative behaviors associated with swipe culture: ghosting, catfishing, gaslighting, dick pics, breadcrumbing, and love bombing. Well over half of my interactions start out either innocent or a little saucy, but then morph into more sexualized and borderline scary forms of communication. In fact, deception, coercion, and misogyny run through my dating app interactions so often that it sometimes feels like a countdown to disappointment from the moment I match with someone. It's eerie how often it works like this, no matter what I do or how I behave.

This reflects the violence and gendered inequities that keep our patriarchal society afloat. It also echoes the anemic and contradictory dialogues we have about sexuality and dating. This important point is rarely explored in relation to dating apps because they are routinely assigned a pathetic-yet-essential gloss or are rendered juvenile. The fact that folks still jab moralistic fingers at these platforms reveals how slow we are to accept and make cultural sense of the revolutionary impact that they're having on relationship dynamics and how we find love, sex, and even community.

Some technologies make aspects of our life smarter, but this isn't always the case. Sometimes all technology can offer is a new package through which our existing vulnerabilities can shape-shift and inside which unresolved undercurrents can flow. We need to talk about what it's like to use these devices; we don't know what we're doing on them and what a lot of us are doing isn't working. It's also very unkind and dead unsexy. The reality of dating apps creeping into and across other digital platforms is also disconcerting. It makes it seem like dating is everywhere, which might sound like heart-shaped fun but it's bewildering to be swarmed by amorous strangers who slip into other digital spaces of my life.

A question that is rarely asked is why are people using all of these new spaces to connect in this particular way? There are a bazillion dating apps and lifestyle clubs designed for all things intimate, why take over my Facebook or Instagram? Is Meta trying to harvest data for its dating app? Or is it a reflection of the global famine we are experiencing in the realm of love and human connection, which is directly tied to the rise of digital culture and practices? These are fascinating questions that I consider in more detail in the pages to come.

But now, the sex, which is the focus of chapter 2.

TWO

Sex in Swipedom

The intolerable Nurse Ratched doorbell shocks me out of my writing groove. Peering at the figure in the glass foyer entrance, it's still not clear who has rung my bell. I slowly open the door and a gangly young man introduces himself as a sales representative who's here for my demonstration. Demonstration? A long vacuum hose, brushes, bags of filters, and a clipboard are jostling around in his thin arms like an assortment of octopi. He wears a black t-shirt, black loafers, and dark jeans with the pockets slung too low, like when "Shape of My Heart" was a hit for the Backstreet Boys. Although his dark brown helmet hair is also pretty dated, something becomes unclutched as I watch him climb the stairs to my apartment.

Why I would have agreed to this sales demonstration is beyond me, especially because I have hardwood and tile flooring in my suite and only a couple of small rugs. I'm a broom and dustpan girl. Dixon introduces himself and then runs back to his vehicle to get the air filter that's part of the exclusive offer. He spreads the equipment out on my dining room floor like a jigsaw puzzle and tells me that the whole operation will take a couple of hours. "You've got to be kidding!" I say with a smile while perched on the edge of the wicker loveseat. He grins and begins talking about pollution containers, superior cleaning attachments, and how these products remove 99.98 per cent of dirt and dust.

Fabric sheets measuring 3" × 3" are pulled out of his bag, sprayed with solvent, and rubbed on various surfaces to reveal the galaxy of microscopic filth I inhale each day. Giggles escape me as he performs these acts of salesmanship, which go on and on. When I wail about how long it's taking and ask if we can cut it short, Dixon says he only gets paid if he completes the full script. In between official information, he drops wildly inappropriate comments about the length of the black hose and tells me three things that make life worthwhile: "Beer, pizza, and sex." We howl in the absurdity and heavy flirting; it's part of the magic. The return of the other half of my sawed-off body that I let slip beneath the stage for too long.

When he slides the three-ply carbon copy receipt towards me, I gasp, not because of the ridiculous amount of money I'm about to spend, but because of his writing. The jaggedy letters dangle on the form where he's printed my name, address, and the cost of the vacuum and the air filter. It reminds me of the banners that hang above the chalkboard in primary grade classrooms to teach children how to write cursively. The rounded capital "A" that takes up a full line and the pear-shaped little "a" that only reaches the dotted half-way mark. He's pressed so hard that the paper curls up in protest, or maybe it's in celebration of his first sale. I've popped a couple of cherries before, but this is my first door-to-door adventure. On this occasion, it's not me who opens new fruit. Instead, I'm reminded to get growing after a twelve-month spread of celibacy.

This outrageous experience catapults me from the year of closed legs to the season of now, when my mojo rises again. How joyful it is to feel attractive and share sensual energy with someone, even a barely legal vacuum and air filter salesman. Being off sex and dating is tough but vital to my emotional well-being following my last relationship, which was abusive and intertwined with many traumas that are beginning to unravel, in a good way. But woman cannot live on healing alone. Nothing says it's time to get back into the game like dropping 5K on home sanitation. It's kind of pricey as a dating strategy though.

I'm not quite ready for the bar scene and live in a small city with few places to meet cool guys, so dating apps it is. They're synonymous with so-called casual sex and, given my predigital dating success, I expect that finding the amorous attention I want should be a piece of cake. Maelina Frattaroli, a.k.a. the Tiny Buddha, says a few things about the word "should." Mainly that it's a term we use when we don't accept reality and it reflects a lack of self-acceptance. These sentiments resonate with some of my sexual interludes on dating apps, especially the grueling work that is required to make spicy times happen. Have I lost my groove?

As an attractive woman living in a society that tells us that what men want is sex, I am baffled. The guys I match with say that getting busy is a priority, but then they often seem content to sext and get anxious when I suggest an in-person meeting. Some are also a bit judgy about the fact that I want to get sweaty between the sheets, which makes me wonder what decade I'm in. Isn't this the era of the hookup? A handful of guys manage to find their way into my eager arms and two of these evolve into meaningful relationships. But these wins are so rare that I'm left wondering when and why physical intimacy got so hard.

Our withered vocabulary about sexuality, gender, power, and how to use dating platforms effectively plays into these struggles. So does the overreliance on swiping because, contrary to what they're marketed as, dating apps often widen the gaps between people instead of bringing us together. The new products (e.g., AI dolls, the fifty-vibration-setting Man Wand) and terms (e.g., kittenfishing, zombie-ing) that pop up daily can also make modern dating hard to understand and experience in the ways we'd like to. This tangle of interconnected issues comes up in almost every conversation I have with fellow dating-app swipesters, but they're hidden or ignored in the social media and marketing messages about how easy it is to connect sexually in Swipedom.

In this chapter I attempt to decipher what sex means within the context of swipe culture. How are dating apps flipping the sexual script? How do I navigate these complex and often disappointing experiences? Has Eros, that winged god of love, forsaken us? It's not just me who cares about the answers to these questions. Many men I encounter on dating apps care too, and they often flag celebrity culture, where everyone is jacked and tucked, and the #MeToo movement as things that make it tough for them to express their desires. Sex seems as hard for them to get as it is for me. Before wading through my reflections and experiences of dating apps and sex, let's peek into the past when the path to intimacy looked a lot different than it does today.

An Analog Interlude

"Men went from being people you could easily trust to being on the periphery," said Joan, my counselor, about the years between my late teens and my twenties. "Yes," I said. During my twenties, in particular, I burn through men. There are a few boyfriends, but nothing significant. Serious relationships aren't something I aspire to because most of the adults around me are in unions defined by emotional turmoil. In this era of grunge and gangsta rap the cauldron bubbles, toils, and is fairly troubled. I stir in some new men, a couple of women, some new positions, a few different places, and a slurry of feelings about myself and sex.

Alongside the regrettable and messy, there are weird and wonderful experiences too, like when a guy I flirt with on a train proposes to me two weeks later. In a letter that includes a very DIY photo of himself outside of a mall, he asks, "Treena will you be my wife?" I run the three blocks to my best friend's house, the letter waving in my hand like a small white flag. As we laugh our heads off in the living room, her mother, who's smoking and reading a novel at the kitchen table, looks on in disbelief and says: "You girls."

Getting a fieldful of white daisies delivered to my apartment after a memorable night with a beautiful woman who works at a record store stands out, too. The card has the most gorgeous message: "Daisies daisies everywhere, their beauty reminds me of you." Then there are the late nights of partying with countless indie and blues bands in the small smoky rooms above the bars on 10th Street in Saskatoon. It is pure 1990s and our thirst for adventure and high tolerance for alcohol pave the way for many wild times.

Moving through these experiences, I am acting out my own subtext about who I am as a sexual woman. Of the many things I feel, accomplishment is high on the list. While writhing between the covers, especially with the really beautiful men, I think "I GOT THEM." I get to touch and marvel at their gorgeous bodies, faces, cocks, and eyes. I get to taste their beauty. I am learning about pleasure as well as myself, and rebelling against the idea that "easy" women give sex or their dignity away; it doesn't feel like that to me, at least not all of the time.

There's nothing like lying next to someone after you've been inside one another, when the make-up is long gone, and the morning may have come. You're united in the smells and feelings you create together. It's singularly intimate. These people are evidence of more than my questionable reputation; they hang around, they share themselves, and sometimes we meet up again. Most of them enjoy being with me for more than the sex, and I feel the same way about most of them. "Casual" sex isn't something to be scraped away from the body like a leech off an ankle. It's there for a reason; you just have to find it.

One of the most momentous encounters I have is with Vance, one of the most gorgeous people I've ever seen. He has the chiseled body of a swimmer, one who also bikes, plays basketball, and has an eating disorder. The man is shredded. I learn about the eating part later, and it makes him even more compelling to me. This god doesn't think he's a god. Vance's face is slightly angular, and he often wears his hair in a loose ponytail, with a few wavy brown tendrils hanging down. His seemingly carefree smile is utterly captivating.

We have sex on my custom futon bed that's covered in a faux Mexican blanket and second-hand pillows. He is as good as you might imagine and while we intertwine, I wonder what he's thinking. How do I compare to the gorgeous women he's had? Is he worried about how his body looks or sounds? I lick the bottom of his feet, something I've never done to anyone before. I can still see the silhouette of his muscular back, arched in delight, as he absorbs the sensations. On his way out, I give him my favorite poetry collection, *A Red Carpet for the Sun*, by Irving Layton, who was a mentor to Leonard Cohen.

When he calls a day or two later, I don't recognize his voice. He says it's "Vance" but that doesn't help too much because there is, oddly, more than one of those at the time. We both pause when it's obvious that I don't recognize him, but then I do. He gets off the phone as fast as he can, and I think the scenario surprises more than hurts him. But I'll never know for sure because we never see each other again. I'm at home when he slides the book under my door, and for a moment I consider saying something. I choose to remain silent and wonder if he read any of the poems.

As Joan and I talk, I envision a row of men lined up along the windowsill. So many empty bottles, uncollected. They magnify and help me understand how I learn to maneuver inside the world of sex, unspoken traumas, and the puzzle of myself during this formative time of life. I collect these memories and then blow the dust away. Sand and heat make glass, and it's also what our phone screens are made of. We glaze these surfaces with our human oils throughout the day; what lies beneath in the kingdom of the swipe and how does it compare to my analog days?

Dating Apps Are Flipping the Sexual Script

While filling out the paperwork at a tattoo shop (Are you breastfeeding? Do you take medications? Are you over eighteen? etc.) I blurt out my burning question to the skinny old-soul dude rolling around on the office chair behind the desk: "Sooo, people don't use dating apps just to date?" He imparts the wisdom that I now know to be true: "Nah nah, they on it for all reasons!" People use them to waste time when they're on public transit or waiting in line somewhere, and many folks are just curious to "see who's out there."

As the Toronto hippie on Queen Street continues to talk I shake my head from side to side in confusion and gratitude. These insights help me reassemble the scattered pieces of information I've been picking up about why and how guys use dating apps, especially when it comes to sex.

People definitely date and want to meet one another, but because these aims are not exclusive among all users it makes sense that the in-person sex I am seeking is sometimes so hard to find. Even guys whose profiles say "interested in meeting new people" might not want to meet at all. Why carry on the charade if they're only swiping because they're bored? Are we pixelating away our ability to think about one another with compassion? Or am I the chump for trying to compare my Jurassic Park dating experiences with what's going on in the digital era? Maybe it's a 2.0 version of the late 1990s proverb: Don't hate the player, hate the game.

Whatever it is, I'm endlessly astounded by the preference for digital versus embodied pleasure. Guys will gleefully text for a few hours or even days, send and request spicy photos, and vanish when I mention meeting. This happens less on Tinder than when I'm on Bumble, yet it remains a constant feature of dating app swipe culture. Do men not want to have sex? Maybe they're using dating apps too much, which can reinforce sexting as an acceptable behavior, often instead of physical sex.

The anxiety about in-person meetings is fundamentally connected with the way dating apps are restructuring traditional dating practices. They are turning what a lot of Gen Xers and other older folks consider to be normative behaviors upside down. By normative, I mean things like bar pickups and meeting people in the wild, which is how dating worked before swiping. In this primordial terrain, in-person encounters are the first and the most common way to connect with someone, whether at a club, work, or through friends. People met online in the 1980s and 1990s, but in minuscule numbers compared to the global uptick since dating apps.

In the dot matrix times, first base is the initial meeting, where some low-key kissing or holding hands might transpire. Second base involves some heavy petting, like a guy going up your shirt or down your pants: note the gendered dating lingo. Third base is a heavier version of second base and penetrative sex might be in the cards. Having sex the first time you meet qualifies as a one-night stand. Although the old-timey, hetero, male-oriented baseball metaphors are cringey, I use them because they are part of the cultural dialogue that informs what dating is when my friends and I come of age.

On digital platforms, the scripts we need to interpret the dating environment and locate ourselves within the mystic universe of sex are being radically transformed. The dating process is far less predictable than in the past, when, for me at least, the booze + bar = sex equation is very dependable. This isn't always the best decision, but I usually know what to expect.

Now, the opening conversation on the app constitutes first base and that's often as far as it goes. Second base is when users transition from the app to regular phone texting or online platforms like Snapchat, which some researchers call the "ritual of transition." This stage involves sending photos and sexting, which can be fun, but a kiss emoji is not a kiss. Third base is the in-person meet up, which is the least frequent outcome on dating apps. The way these steps play out varies a lot and depends on the platform being used, the number of fish in the sea, and whether there's, say, a global pandemic happening, which slows everyone's roll for a while.

Sometimes the speed of the swipe, the anonymity, and the sexually charged nature of the hunt, where nothing is guaranteed, is fun. But romance as secret entertainment, where everything lives and dies within our phones, is also a little creepy. So too is the surveillance aspect of swiping. Most phone-operated apps are designed with GIS technology that determines not only who's "out there" but also where they are. The location feature can be turned off or altered to report any city or country, which creates a feast of spatial speculation. I regularly use this feature to see where my dates are before, or instead of, communicating with them.

This is so far removed from knowing where a date was in the 90210 days, when the most you could hope for is for him to pick up the phone or show up at the same place you were. The GIS function produces another outcome that's different from the days of acid wash and TV theme song playlists – remember those? With each new kilometer traveled, a new sea of potential fish is revealed. This is mobile romance, which is nothing like analog times when I date people from the same neighborhood or city. I have sexual adventures in places other than where I live, but they are one-offs directed by human chance, not an algorithm.

When I first begin swiping, I include Toronto in my catchment area to take advantage of the big city guys who are way cooler than what's available in my bumpkin city. A longish distance relationship isn't necessarily attractive to me, but I'll make it work for the right guy. There's lots of interest from men in "the Six," as Toronto is known, but because they literally never leave downtown – it's not just an urban myth – they're not a viable option. I'm doubly damned by geography because the local offerings are meager and the enticing guys in the Six don't leave the city perimeter. Who can I date?

I admit defeat and take Toronto off my dating radar, but before shutting it down completely I follow up on an interesting match in the big city. My fieldnotes capture some of the tensions I feel about what I'm doing and why:

It's 6:50 a.m. and I'm standing in the foyer of my building after a snowstorm. A stream of cold air comes through the heavy front door, and I look at the hunks of snow clustered along the quiet, dark streets. Is it pathetic, doing this for sex? Is this prostitution? It would seem to fit most basic definitions: an exchange of material items/goods for sexual services/experiences. I shrug my shoulders and bound out the door when I see the taxi, which is white and almost camouflaged against the snow. What do you do? This is what I want, and this is what I'm doing to get it.

Navigating Sexual Experiences on Dating Apps

This segment of the program is called "I know what I want but not what I'm doing." People laugh when I tell them how long it takes to figure out dating apps. Have *you* ever tried to master them while chasing a dozen guys who sext screenfuls of porn and emojis every minute? It's more than the nuts and bolts of these platforms and how men use them that stupefy me. I scramble to make sense of how I'm responding to this vacuous, yet also enticing, environment. Sometimes I feel hopeless about the fact that misogyny and moralizing dialogues about women who enjoy sex are often the order of the day.

At other times, I like surrendering to the swipe machines in our palms. Letting my PC guard down and interacting with guys I'd never meet any other way allows me to see deeper into their lives and the intersecting issues of gender, power, and digital communication. A sense of discovery runs through almost every match I make, which helps answer one of the questions I get asked often: "Why do you keep using these things?" It's because I'm a horny nerd who's committed to the pursuit of pleasure and finding interesting people to include in my intimate life.

Also, I don't just meet weird and infuriating men. I've had the delicious fortune to connect with many beautiful and interesting men, too. They bring fun and new experiences to the table, along with just the right combination of confidence and vulnerability. And sex, they also bring sex. Before showing you what all of this looks like in my dating app life, here's a poem. I wrote it several years ago after saying "Have a good day!" to a lover as he left my apartment. Saying such a formal thing feels awkward, but there is something else, a kind of hope, encoded in these words:

> *I like you*
> *Come back*
> *Manners seem strange*
> *Considering what we*
> *Just released*
> *Mouths agape*
> *Shiny bodies sway*
> *The pull of pink*
> *After, I kiss his neck*
> *He says, "Thank you."*

Baby-oh-baby

The jacked-up guy with the eagle chest tattoo looks like a whole lotta man. His selfies are mainly at the gym, which is kind of boring, and the eagle looks slightly too small for the meaty space it resides on, but I can live with it. Boo is very eager, but then he goes all chastity belt and begins asking questions that make me feel like I'm at a drive-in with Jughead. I literally scream when I see these questions come across my screen:

"Do you have sex with lots of guys?"
"When was the last time you had sex?"
"Was it random?"
"Do you chat with other dudes while dating or talking to
    other guys?"

It's a sunny day in double-standard land, make sure to wear
your sunglasses 'cause the judgment is bright. "Define lots,"
"none of your business," "yes," and "sometimes." I'm on
a DATING APP and so are you. After telling him what he
wants to hear ("no," "a while ago," "no," "rarely") he says
that I should be freaky and fun, but only with him. Um,
we don't even know each other and I'm not yours to boss
around. This exchange is ridiculous and offensive, but yet it
feels so familiar. Women go through these sexist, patriarchal
hoops so often it barely registers as wrong. Does he even
believe what I'm saying? Is any of this real?

    After bailing on our original date and deleting me from
the app, he tells me he's "OMW." I'm flabbergasted that
he's driving ninety minutes in the rain to get here. Fingers
crossed he looks like his selfies, which I freely share with
a few friends. "OMG Treena, he's gorgeous," one woman
says. "SCORE," I reply! His ripped body delivers as prom-
ised, but I can't get over how terribly tight his clothes are. I
haven't seen jeans like this since scrolling through pictures
of Robert Plant c. 1969, à la "The Lemon Song." The surface
of his skin looks coarser than in the pictures – men use filters too – and he's nervous.

    He comes at me with mouth and his hands and his words:
"You're so beautiful, mmmmmm, mmmmmmm." We

scamper down the hallway and in the candlelight, with the faint scent of basil and neroli wafting, I take in the body I've been hungrily wondering about all week. It looks identical to the desired V-frame splashed across *Men's Health* magazine – broad shoulders, tapered waist. But I don't think he knows how to move his body beyond the bench press, the office, and normal man activities. I am somehow absent.

Is he disassociating? I literally don't think he looks at me once while making spicy declarations and uncreative physical motions. He says the phrase "baby-oh-baby" a few times and I have to clamp my lips tightly to prevent the cackle from escaping. I look at him, aghast, and decide to just focus on keeping pace. I'm like a fly on the wall of my own encounter, rubbing my front legs together to roll out this story.

As he prepares to leave, I provide a glass of water and some idle chitchat. Then out of nowhere, he grabs me by the midsection and lifts me into the air. I let out a piglet squeal. Stiffly suspended in his arms that prickle with hair growing in after a shave, I survey the world above the IKEA table and chairs. I don't look down because it's too weird. Is he looking at me? If he is, I bet it looks like a vintage advertisement that features twirling girls in parachute skirts and men with exaggerated dimples and dirty blonde cartoon hair grinning at them.

Back on solid ground, I walk him to the door as he chats happily about the date. "It was worth it," he says, referring to the hour and a half drive. I nod agreeably and watch him labor to tie his boots up. "This weekend?" he asks eagerly, to which I reply in an even tone: "We'll be in touch." One final wet kiss goodbye and he zooms away. Coming back into my apartment I look at my cats wide-eyed and ask, "Whaat was that?" Laying on my bed wearing a t-shirt and underwear, I survey my room: bedside table lamp, Jo Malone candle, jewelry, clothes, art, pieces of my life.

All these things have interacted with a man whose last name I do not know and have no interest in learning. It's so strange and fascinating but turns ugly when I tell him I'm not into another date. His texts go from cute to ridiculing and it ends with: "lol ... OK then." His juvenile response is the biggest turnoff. It makes me feel dumb for spending the limited amount of time with him that I did. He was fine, weird but fine, at my place but it's like there was someone else inside all along, a mean guy, a man for whom the word no does not register. We're all performing, I guess, including me.

The Man with the Soft Hair

Hmmm, he looks softer than in the photos, not just his flesh but also his hair. It feels extremely soft. This includes his facial hair, the stuff on his forearms, and even the hair that gathers richly along his legs. I don't normally like a lot of fur, but this is different. I look at his body gyrating into my own and then glance quickly at his face to read the signs of pleasure. How to describe them? Finding the words feels impossible, like trying to describe color.

How do you talk about what blue looks like, anyway? Men's faces, during sex, reflect a range of emotions – the physical work of sex, the pained joy of sensual release, the greediness of good pleasure. The same must be true of mine in certain situations. The fusion of two bodies, an embodied assemblage. As Hedwig of *Hedwig and the Angry Inch* says, sex is about putting ourselves together. What is being created in moments like this, between people who have never seen one another before and will likely never see one another again?

Fun, excitement, good body feelings, a firing up of the brain's pleasure and reward circuits, connection? Sometimes, it's also about the prospect of something more. These thoughts flash across my mind as I meet his eyes momentarily and then return to my own body.

The orgasm gap is alive and well in this encounter and almost all of them with new people who are only in my bed once. Providing sexual instruction is a form of labor, and if I'm not too turned on it won't yield the desired result. This man isn't terribly sexually attractive to me and there is no magic button to simply "press" for desired results. Yet, he's one of the only men who seems curious about the fact that I don't climax. I appreciate his concern, but playing with myself is something I usually do with my close partners. Plus, I have a toy handy for when he leaves.

Afterwards we chat about our favorite writers, books, and the craft of writing. Instead of pouring my knowledge of these subjects into the heads of less curious men, it's lovely to have a mutually illuminating conversation about issues that mean a lot to both of us. Our conversation drifts into the dining room and I hear myself offering life advice instead of replying to questions about things I'm interested in. This feels a little like the "teacher" and "student" mode I'm used to at work, which isn't nearly as hot as most people think it is.

Still, I'm intrigued that he is curious about my insights as a successful, well-traveled, fairly balanced woman. He's not the first younger guy (fourteen years younger than my forty-five years) who's hot for me, specifically, as an older woman. But am I just a cougar-ific catch on his sexual bucket list? He tells me that he's interested in learning about my struggles, including alcohol and earlier traumas, and how I find my way in a demanding profession at a school with a reputation for being an old boys' club.

He too has gone through a lot in his relatively young life and doesn't have many safe, informative spaces within which he can let his guard down and ask for guidance about how to navigate these experiences. Being appreciated for who I am as well as my erotic capital contrasts with the dominant social view of older women as either sexually undesirable or pathetic. It teaches me that there are young men out there who want to buck the unforgiving patriarchal system as much as I do.

Embodying the "millennial shift," which refers to changing sexual and lifestyle aims among younger generations, this guy wants to try on a new kind of masculinity. He's not really interested in marriage or having a single partner throughout his life, and he is searching for another way of being a person in the world. Although he's not a romantic prospect going forward, the exchange of ideas we have is lovely and feels empowering for both of us.

The evening draws to a close and I walk him down the hallway, where he pauses at the back door, wanting, I think, for me to give him a sign that there will be more. He makes a joke about not wanting to fuck me over but wanting to fuck me again. Out of the side of my body, I watch him assess me and quietly digest my basic but not encouraging response. I open the door a crack, give him a quick hug and say

"Yep, you go down there," pointing to the door that leads to the stairwell. He smiles and walks towards it.

Fantasy Island: Swiping in Sicily

There are places that plant themselves in me the moment I touch down, and Palermo is one of them. Giddy with jetlag and the spectacular Le Madonie mountain range, which is the color of rust and butter icing in the evening sun, I am enthralled by the time I get to my Airbnb. In the backseat of the taxi, I take my first selfie of the trip and am struck by the jubilant gloss of my skin from the tropical temperatures and the freedom of being somewhere new. I already look in love.

My host texts me to say he'll be a few minutes late, which I don't mind because it gives me a chance to drink in the extravagant Baroque church across the street, the sounds of people talking to one another, and to gaze as far as my eyes can see along the cobweb of cobblestone streets. When he arrives I feel like a peon and wish I was wearing something other than a tank top and leisure pants. He is so gorgeous all I can do is smile and follow him quietly inside. It's unlike any building I've seen before, and the modern apartments seem to be implanted in the carved-out husk of the centuries-older exterior structure.

After heaving my huge bag inside we travel up a glass elevator to the second floor. The host quickly gives me a tour and, in between some sexy pauses in our conversation, I'm pretty sure that something is going to happen. But how?

On this small island, my luck is ripe and when I come across my host's profile on Tinder a few minutes later I swipe right without thinking. When in Palermo, right? Hilariously, he replies to my message seconds later, saying, "Hello Treena, I am your host" – yeah, I know! Once we establish that we're interested in meeting, he tells me that he's very busy and will message me tomorrow. Ciao!! It's still light and I have a few hours of life in me, so I continue swiping and have a few hilarious exchanges with guys whose English is less than perfect:

> HIM: Ciao, you are here in vacancy? You are alone?
> ME: Yes, here for a week. Up for some fun soon.
> HIM: Ah, ok. But what you search here? I like however sex.

> ME: Hello! I'm a university professor from Canada, here for vacay.
> HIM: Nice ... I'm sorry I can not speak English. However, congratulations you are very charming.

I arrange to meet a local policeman, whose sexy confidence and okay English are the ticket tonight. It's cool and weird to walk around with a hot guy who barely speaks the same language but knows what's up. Pasta, gelato, and then we are at my place for some Sicilian lovin'. I'm exhausted and elated when I finally tuck in for some sleep under the duvet in my beautiful little abode. What an adventure already!

Over the next week, I have passionate sex with my host several times, which leaves me deliriously in lust. On the third date he says, "I love you," which sets in motion a dramatic sequence of events that involves a lot of pining. Although neither of us is really in love, we say it to one another repeatedly while weeping under the stars about how unfair geography is. My girlfriends encourage me to follow my feelings and to return the next chance I can. They urge me on by saying things that are ludicrous but exactly what I want to hear, things like "You can write books in Sicily, how romantic!" and "What a triumph of dating apps!"

He's excited for a return trip, too. A hot chick from halfway around the world coming back to him, who wouldn't be up for that? Yet my heart is a tricky machine that sometimes forgets the emotional rollercoaster that accompanies this fiendish approach to romance.

I return home a woman changed by that magical volcanic island near the toe of Italy's boot. I excitedly book a flight for October with the assistance of an Australian woman at the travel agency. I tell her the loin-moistening details and she's soon a member of team Sicily, too! But when I share my itinerary with my former host, he is silent. In the strange hours that only jetlag offers, I jot these reflections while juggling hope and fear in the wordless air:

I gnaw my way through the spoils of a fiery Sicilian summer and traipse through milky clouds that streak the azure sky above Palermo. There's the domed cathedral with its motley Spanish-Norman-Moorish architecture, the majestic Teatro Massimo, and the Villa Bonanno gardens in the city's most ancient zone – my favourite place on earth.

I see bustling Via Milano with its wide slippery stones the color of ancient snake. The nighttime corners come into view, where you feed me strawberry marzipan and smoke in the moonlight while the sugar slips around in my mouth. "Anything is possible," I say; "everything is possible," you say.

How quickly things transpire from that singular purpose of getting inside one another to the swampy steps beyond the fragile unity of sex.

Sex brings me things I want, but it never comes clean. Bodies have people inside them that are made of sinew, many teeth with long roots, and they run with blood that moves in two directions. The flesh stores all.

Two days later and still no message; it feels like forever. It always does when your breath is dependent upon someone else who filters this dusty world like a tree. Mortified, I cancel my flight and want to get my money back, which means I have to provide the insurance company with a legitimate reason or complaint. Choking back tears to the nice man at the end of the 1-800 number I say the first thing that comes to mind: "coercion."

He doesn't skip a beat and informs me that I must provide some evidence and that, yes, screenshots of his promises and outraged texts with my friends when he ghosts me will suffice. I successfully retrieve about 85 per cent of the plane ticket costs and then the man in Palermo texts back.

Three months later I'm in my cherished Sicily once again. I bound down the familiar streets, hot with Mediterranean energy and my new caramel-colored leather tote. The Sicilian proverb "Cu nesci arrinesci" (Who leaves their own comfort zone succeeds) is my mantra. Along with my former lover, whose work schedule allows him to see me for just one hour, I meet a thrilling new guy. He instructs me to remove my underwear as I climb the steps to his apartment and says that when I enter his apartment I'll find a surprise. By the light of a tiny burning candle, I discover him with a bandana over his eyes and an array of toys on the bed. Let's do this!

I even see the policeman again; he asks "How are things in Ireland?" I scream and say, "I'm from Canada" and we both roll around the bed laughing our guts out. October is a bit cooler than July and so there are lots of holiday tour buses full of folks with white hair. It doesn't slow my roll one bit, and I do fun things I didn't do last time. I ride in a dilapidated carriage pulled by a graying horse, I visit the Capuchin catacombs full of centuries-old dead people who are lovingly cared for, and I eat cannoli instead of marzipan.

From Zero to Sixty in Twenty-One Months

Treena, 48 (University professor)
<u>Tinder goals</u> – casual, something meaningful, open to
   possibilities
<u>Tinder likes</u> – fit, healthy, kind, smart, funny, imaginative,
   meet in-person (blue "COOL" emoji)
<u>Tinder dislikes</u> – not reading my profile, objectification, lazy
   or careless communication, boring questions about sexual
   preferences, text-only (monkey covering eyes emoji)
<u>Bonus</u> – animals, travel, reading and the arts, independent,
   originality (gold trophy emoji)

Treena, 49 (University professor)
Why bother using this anymore … no one wants to meet
   (face emoji with eyes rolling)?

Treena, 49 (University professor)
A little bit of kindness goes a long way, we're still going
   through it (strawberry and heart emoji)
Double-vaxxed (syringe emoji)

Ah, my three pandemic profile write-ups – ebb-anguish-flow. Thanks to a Tinder-induced relationship that's just fizzled out, it's been over a year since my last swipe. Deep in the synapses that spurt information between body and brain, I know that sex and meaningful connection are wild cards at this foreign and scary time. But I go for them anyway. The term "skin hunger" emerges early in the pandemic to describe the yearning many of us have for human touch, which is often unrequited. This word sends shivers up all my vertebrae, like when I hear "white walker" in *Game of Thrones*. How close we will come to the North Wall?

I match with a bunch of guys, but they go nowhere for reasons that feel like the usual dating app drama, but there's something else behind the standstill. Global trauma and an unprecedented sense of not knowing what's next. It's not just men who are being "flaky" (and it's so much more than that): I am too. We're all slumped inside our homes just pressing life's buttons. I want to reach out but feel like I should conserve my energies to navigate our new reality, the rules and regulations of the next phase, and new behaviors that have yet to be named.

Everything is on hold. Where does dating fit when most of us are coveting toilet paper, designing new offices that sprout up around the house, and storing away jars of fear?

Images of atomic bomb mushroom clouds come to mind, how beautiful and impressive they are. The pictures I've seen of them are almost all the same: gigantic white plumes that look both phallic and fungi-like reaching into clear blue skies. There's a fictional, floaty sense of serenity, like time has evaporated. COVID-19 is like this. For two years the eight billion souls living on this planet we call home have been living, and dying, under a very big cloud.

In these uncharted times, dolphins return to the canals in Venice, and we swipe on dating apps in record numbers. Video dates are introduced, which sounds boring but potentially juicy. I never do one, though. My kingdom for a gloryhole! But wait, my loins are drained of all romantic confidence and desire. Or are they just in cruise control? Dating and wanting to date feels absurd, like leaving the lights on when you're not at home. Except I am at home, I'm here all the time and nothing feels right. That must be why so many of us are quietly going berserk in Swipedom and why so many guys say "I'm not on here that often."

Dating during a pandemic seems to be about showing our vulnerability to one another. To see how much we can navigate from inside our respective shells and what is worth taking on. As I see it, there are five options when traffic is at a virtual crawl: feeling like crap about myself, playing harder, lowering my standards, uninstalling the app, or idling. Turns out, I'm a master idler.

Idle *verb*
1 (of a person) spend time doing nothing; be idle. "Four
   men were idling outside the shop."
       do nothing, be inactive, vegetate, take it
           easy, mark time, twiddle one's thumbs, kill
           time, languish, laze, lounge, loll, loaf, loiter;
       informal – hang around, veg out, bum around, lollygag
   "Treena idled on Tinder and then wrote about it."

What I want feels like a moving target that's based on the quality not only of the fish in the current sea but of the sea itself. An estuary might be more apt. A partially enclosed coastal body of water with one or more rivers or streams flowing into it, an estuary has free connections to the ocean and is a transitional zone between river and maritime environments. That sounds right: transition, salty and fresh, open to larger possibilities.

Hundreds of profiles still come my way. Some make me sad and confused, so many love bombers mingled with unvaccinated incels. Some make me randy and then mad because they're hot, but they disappear – where'd you go with my hard-on? – or don't answer my messages. I explore other options including paying for sex. Sweet Jesus, no. There are guys with the right equipment in the vicinity, but from their service descriptions they sound more like rent boys than polished escorts. I scroll through my alma mater, Craigslist, too, but it's basically one guy posting five identical messages about wanting to provide "oral to women."

What about creating business cards to distribute to potential suitors? How about the Foxy Feminist? I think of this name while going on yet another boring walk around the block one night. I chicken out with the cards; my balls aren't blue enough to do it. Plus, the name is used by a lot of other people. Swiping feels like a textbook case of the sunk cost fallacy, with me doggedly pouring time and energy into something I know is a sinking ship. Remaining sad and unsexed is awful and try as I may to tuck these thorny feelings away, they never retreat for long.

Oracle cards, yoga, and coffee dates with colleagues just aren't enough. I feel damned as well as deserving, so I carry on. Resources, meet ocean floor.

It's even more ridiculous when I look at the guys I'm chatting with, most of whom embody what I call "millennial meh." After the initial spark of speedy messages, the interest dips below the freezing point; this despite providing me their digits to, ostensibly, continue the conversation. The same stunted weirdness circulates through my chats with fellow Gen X men, like the sober, yoga-oriented dad who is also a Sagittarius. We have some engaging exchanges, but when I ask what he's looking for he says, "I don't take online dating seriously."

Okay, so you enjoy swiping and chatting whenever for no real purpose, me not so much. I delete him after days of silence on his end and when he adds this to his profile: "If you're vaxxed, swipe left. Careful, your phone has germs."

Finally, a dating success. I'm very rusty, but the two of us show up and that feels like a win. We walk through the park way too fast and have a rather stilted conversation, but it feels nice to actually hear and see a man walking beside me. A second date is planned, which goes less well. I'm more interested in the waitress than the guy, who talks about, among other things, his buddy "banging some chick in the bathroom." Then there's a well-rounded European who likes cats and friend-zones me after our second date, which was fun and sexy. He sends me this lameness: "I'm very busy this month and it doesn't look like it will improve next month … I hope you understand."

The pandemic seal is finally broken in August 2021 with a guy whose selfies all show him surfing or posing with a surfboard, eight hard abs on full display. He definitely does beach. There's nothing like a sexual reawakening, especially when it's fun and promises are made about a next time. But there is no round two because he ghosts me. I'm floored, yet again, as captured in my fieldnotes recorded a few weeks after we meet.

Where does the wisdom go when you let yourself let someone else in? Sometimes it hides behind the bright, bossy, wetness of desire. It also floats inside the apps, my mind, and their bodies, balancing precariously between the molecules of lust and fear that bind us together. Knowing your worth doesn't mean you'll ever achieve it. So, I keep drifting from one swipe of my thumb to another. Onward I travel; surveying the men I've scaled and sought like an amateur mountaineer.

The words from your mouth stick to my head like pollen on the stamen: "You are incredible, perfect." But when you are not here and spare few words, I hear different things. "How could I be so stupid?" "Will my search for what I deserve ever end?" Those old ideas bounce back from my amygdala's cave with such ease. How I wish to bend those filaments of knowledge and desire between my knowing lobes to release new seeds. Maybe that's what I'm doing here with these letters on this screen.

Three months later, right around the time round three of the COVID-19 vaccine is available, I hit my pandemic dating stride. There must be a scientific correlation between vaccines and ecstatic sex because the encounters I have with the next three men are amazing. Maybe I'm feeling more relaxed as we edge closer to our new normal. Maybe more guys who are more interesting are coming out of their homes and into my view.

When I'm out with the first man, I feel attention from other guys but instead of flirting like I used to do, I just meet their gaze and nothing more. I'm glad to see my date when he returns from the restaurant bathroom, but no butterflies are released. We go out a couple more times, but it begins to feel awkward because we don't talk about what we each want. He also sends a few messages that give me passive-aggressive vibes. In a text or two I tell him that I'm not really into how things are shaping up between us, and there seem to be no hard feelings.

The second guy and I are on the same page about what we want from the beginning, and for a few months it's magic. We see one another once a week and always feel desire. But during pillow talk he says things that don't jive with my feminist sensibility, like saying that I look like a schoolteacher on the outside and a bad girl on the inside because of my tattoos and high sexual energy. Sexual desire shouldn't ever be associated with the hidden or the bad sides of women. I hold my breath while lying beside the patriarchy for a few more weeks because he's so good at sex. Things fizzle out when he leaves town, and by then I meet the man in the garden who releases all the fluttery things with each text.

What Is Sex?

From vacuums to vaccines, this chapter lays out the wide-ranging life events that make up my tarot of sex. Like divination cards that are divided into major and minor arcana categories, some of my experiences are shaped by high-level factors (e.g., parents, gender, trauma) and others by more basic issues (e.g., lovers, places traveled, swiping right or left). Whether it's during my rocky ride through early womanhood or the present, I'm curious about how sex shapes my identity and overlaps with the lives of other people. When I think about it a few things come to mind – the exchange of powerful energies, the hot carnal sounds we make, and observing a lover learning how to touch me. The image of red hearts and arrows also surfaces thanks, in part, to the Hallmarkification of Valentine's Day. But Eros, the god whose courageous life is detailed in several ancient Greek texts, also influences the links we make between love and red hearts. Eros means "to desire, to love," and he and his Roman counterpart Cupid have for centuries been associated with bows, arrows, candles, hearts, wings, and kisses. These symbols represent their occupational adventures in the domain of love.

Eros was in love with a mortal called Psyche, meaning "soul, spirit, breath, animating force, or consciousness" according to the Oxford English Dictionary. She was reputed to be so beautiful that only a god could satisfy her, and Eros took up this challenge. For a mortal and a god to get together, a lot of risks were taken for love, which were consecrated through sex. Sex binds the sacred and the profane. It can be divine and worth risking everything for. Pass me my toga. I know it's a story, but glimmers of what is written in these myths remain with us today. Just think of all the songs, stories, movies, poems, and plays that are written about love/ sex/desire/lust. Pour some sugar on me, would ya.

Compare this to the sometimes barren landscape on dating apps, where romance is not a primary aim for all users and sex is often reduced to a digital conversation. Many forms of human communication are digitized and promote watching activities instead of participating in them. This is true of gaming, social media, and pornography, platforms that came before dating apps and consume hours of people's lives each day. This helps explain why a lot of dating app users prefer digital versus in-person interactions.

Swiping platforms also contribute to what Belgian researcher Sander De Ridder calls the "datafication of intimacy," which refers to the mathematical relationship between data economies and intimacy. This is evident in the tremendous amount of time and labor we must invest to secure something more than a sexting partner, and in the way that algorithms and not pheromones guide our romantic paths.

For a Gen X woman raised on hookups and the luck of the dating draw, the datafication of intimacy is about as big a turnoff as there can be, with the exception of misogyny and disliking animals. Flatulence is another big turnoff: "Fart Guy," I'm looking at you. This guy farted in the hallway of my apartment while doing up his shoes after our shit date. He spent most of the date needling me to see if I actually understood the less-than-Einstein points he was making or if I was just nodding my head. He sends this a few days later:

> Just wanted to check in and say that the cats, and the fact that you don't have a car are definitely drawbacks for me. Otherwise I find you very interesting to talk to and definitely a physical attraction.

Noticeably absent from his text is any mention of the fart, not that I expect him to mention it, really. I get this message while getting my hair done, and, after giving the women around me the lowdown of our date, we conclude that I must mention it in my reply. I thank him for the message while pointing out that he didn't mention "the fart." It feels easier to be a little bitchy than unpack how he made me feel on the date, which I know he won't get or will refute. Not my proudest moment, but he wasn't that nice to me either!

Reflecting on the kinds of sex I have with men I meet on dating apps, I find it ranges from semi- to fairly hot, and in some instances it's a sopping masterpiece of pleasure. When it's a kinetic fury of fun and erotic energy I'm reminded that no matter how we come together, by chance or by swipe, Eros hasn't abandoned us. Even on dates when the sex isn't great there can be something valuable gleaned, like learning how many young men are eager to know more about intimacy, female desire, and life in general through the lens of an older woman. They want these things from me because they appreciate my experiences, struggles, and sexual capital.

This is so different from how older women, with the exclusion of the Heidi Klums of the world, are normally thought of when it comes to sex. We're not cougars with fried hair and animal print ensembles or dried up crones whose soft spots have fossilized. Younger men, in particular, are into us. Let's get this narrative into circulation, STAT. As fellow anthropologist and cultural critic Wednesday Martin said, referencing the need for society to pay attention to the beneficial, exciting, and very modern nature of older women and younger men relationships: "Keep up."

Global adventures also accompany my swiping sexual escapades – brava Tinder international! In Sicily there are many times when my wobbly legs have nothing to do with the cobblestones under my feet. Men are hungry for the red-headed tourist in town who's up for some tasty gelato. It's a riot in the best way, and I feel safe, incredibly sexy, and enjoy the earthy intimacy. The fake love story is a bit much, but my sex-lust life has always been dramatic so, really, it all fits!

The pandemic impacts sex and dating apps in many unique and still untold ways. For most of my time under the COVID-19 cloud, sex is something I'm ravenous for and I feel unfairly denied. I become very good at idling and during those stagnant months and years, I imagine sex as a kind of channel. Not like the kind on a TV, but like those 30 miles of track beneath the English Channel that connect Kent, UK, to Calais, France. A passageway from one land to another, from one body to another, a way to survive and scratch together something of the divine. A way to feel alive in the company of another person who is also witnessing the planetary shift we're still recovering from.

Sex is a multi-colored thing that drips lust, hormonal changes, secrets, and sometimes pain. It's the most potent story we tell about one another. It can help us reassemble and make sense of the past, like those bottles on the shelf in Joan's office. Sex is also bound up in intimacy, which is often reserved for the times when we pry open the doors of vulnerability. Sex is a meeting ground and a place to find and express ourselves. It is the ultimate platform and dating apps haven't – not yet anyway – wiped it clean of its animal instincts. What about the interplay between swipe culture and feminism – can there still be sexy times while swiping as a feminist? Find out in chapter 3.

THREE

Feminish

#TreenaOrchard is a cautionary tail of what Feminism has wrought: she's single & childless at 50, pretending to be Carrie Bradshaw while pathetically prowling dating aps. Like so many other feminists, she replaced her aborted child with love for her cats.

Tom J., July 30, 2019 (Twitter)

The author has turned a series of private personal encounters into an anthropological study of a type of creature that's beyond her usual specialization – ordinary men. She sounds to be a bit lost among a tribe that speaks a foreign language.

Max F., July 31, 2019 (The Conversation)

I just read your article in the *National Post*. I believe in gender equality with all my heart. I do not have a single misogynist bone in my body. Yet still, I tell you with all of the passion that I have to muster, that your article is the highest order of delusion.

I would sincerely love, and be grateful for, the opportunity to help you gain a greater understanding of the real dynamics of men and women in the modern world. I believe, respectfully, that every word of the article was too steeped in outdated feminist ideology to be able to help anybody in this modern world. Please do not take the traditional feminist route and dismiss my actions as misogyny, a male unable to cope with the demise of patriarchy, or other feminist stereotypes straight from the feminist Echo chamber. I believe that you have erred profoundly and would like to converse with you on the matter of internet/ app dating. It is my goal that you will eventually recant your assertions in this article, and replace them with ones which are more reasonable, more modern, more effective, and ultimately more able to bring men and women together to live in peace and harmony.

Angus A., August 1, 2019 (Facebook)

I've read these comments many times and yet they still snare me. I laugh and then hold my breath while sinking back into my office chair. Looking out the window, my eyes land on the cedar trees standing at attention and my neighbor's newly reshingled roof. The black asphalt glistens like a tarry mirage in the summer heat.

These men want me to be encased under a ceiling of glass, they wish me to be small, obedient, and weak. There, I feed on polite little meals that will never make me burp and will never nourish me. They want to not just erase me; they want to tread upon my feminist bones. I cry at these words because they're still true across all the dark ages and each soft minute that beats up until now.

Hyped up on promises of empowering, easy connections, I buzz into Bumble, the world's first "feminist" dating app. Beyond a few fun tumbles, life inside the yellow Hive is pretty sexless, which seems weird for a dating platform. Many guys seem to resent the app's design, whereby women make the first move; men must wait to be asked out and many are outright rude. Why are you on here then? It doesn't appear to be about supporting feminism or appreciating women, it's simply a way to maximize their dating success. More apps = more chances. Insert emoji with straight lines for the eyes and mouth.

Six weeks after I join Bumble, Alyssa Milano tweets about being sexually assaulted and encourages people with similar experiences to speak out. She catapults the hashtag #MeToo, first coined by Tarana Burke in 2006 to assist women survivors of sexual assault, especially women of color, into the cultural stratosphere. Women around the world begin unleashing their stories about encounters with sexual violence and the patriarchy buckles under the weight of the fear and anger streaming out of devices, news media, and mouths everywhere.

It's exhilarating and I share things that I've never told anyone. Yet I also feel like the enemy of Man Scorned and as though a tidal wave of harm is waiting for me around the corner. The dual sense of freedom and foreboding grows as counter-hashtags like #notallmen are launched and talk of excluding women from business trips and social activities with male colleagues begins to surface. Using a feminist dating app feels risky and so does dating during this maelstrom.

I begin writing to make sense of dating apps and this unique cultural moment in our stretched-at-its-seams world. The night before submitting my first story about Bumble for publication an intuitive oracle sends me two questions that loop in my head like divebombing swallows: Should I self-identify as a feminist? and How can I not?

My willingness to talk about what it feels like to use this platform, including my critique of Bumble's design and my dating vulnerabilities, hits a nerve. The article is shared on hundreds of websites, blogs, and online forums that promote toxic forms of masculinity and misogyny. In a flash, I'm thrust deep into what is known as the mano-sphere, and I realize that what angers most of the commentators and trolls isn't dating, it's the dreaded F-word. Thus begins my instruction in how feminism is being burned at the digital stake.

For over two decades, I've conducted research about sexuality, gender, and health among marginalized cultural groups. This work puts me in the line of fire as I challenge outdated and oppressive representations of these communities and address controversial issues like sex work. I've been previously harassed, threatened, and stalked, which helps me deal with the online hatred. But these research experiences are no match for the education I receive about feminism from using Bumble and then writing about it. This chapter explores the emotional and intellectual tensions involved in navigating this platform as a feminist, including the scary and compelling things I observe about gender, power, and sex within swipe culture. But first, what *IS* feminism?

Feminism for Life

Primarily concerned with gender identity and expression, and protecting the rights, freedoms, and bodily autonomy of women and other groups who experience exclusion, feminism comes in a crackling array of colors. Contrary to the notion that "all feminists" are women who hate men, have hairy legs, and are angry, some feminists are men, and some are diversely gendered people. The more radical folks adopt binary views of gender and consider male power structures to be the source of all violence against women. Those in the mainstream camps often advocate for equity for all alongside women's rights. Feminism can also be exclusionary and transphobic, in the case of trans-exclusionary radical feminists.

There's no universal consensus, but feminism is premised on the idea that women are human beings entitled to the rights and the opportunities to freely and equally pursue educational, occupational, cultural, and political aspirations. If you're nodding your head, please remember that these ideas are still contested. It remains a battle. We see this in the US Republican Party's backlash against gay marriage, safe abortions, and access to contraception. In many countries, anti-feminist policies have rolled back women's gains in recent years. According to a 2022 UN Women report, gender disparities are worsening, and it could take another 286 years to close the global gender gaps in legal protections for women and girls. That brings us to the year 2309.

Rebecca Solnit writes of these things in her small but mighty book *Men Explain Things to Me*, which opens with a hideous account of "mansplaining." She describes

being at a party where a man waxes on about the merits
of an excellent book that's been recently published. Solnit
wrote the book in question, but each time her friend tries
to share this news with Mr. Very Important he ignores
her. It takes her friend three or four interjections before he
finally stops talking over and at the two women. Many of
us feel this every day.

I grew up as a little feminist on the prairie, inspired by
the American TV drama series about pioneer life in Walnut
Grove, Minnesota. Based on the *Little House on the Prairie*
books by Laura Ingalls Wilder, the series starred Michael
Landon. I was taken with him and his wholesome toothy
grin and radiant black hair, which stood out against the
strawberry blonde locks of the bonneted girl children and
the demure mother. It was always Charles Ingalls for me.

My early feminist sparks flashed brightest with my dad,
who never used "baby talk" and regularly asked for my
input on what I found interesting about certain things, like
a picture in the art gallery or how different groups of people behave. His involvement in Indigenous and left-leaning
circles opened me up to a league of women whose lives
were different from those circulating in mainstream society
in the 1970s and 1980s. No one was married, some worked
as carpenters and didn't shave their body hair, others were
employed at community agencies. They all used the arts as
well as activism to make change in the world. These women
took up a lot of space.

Feminism comprises many stories. In mine there are pages
devoted to exciting and hard-won contributions to different
causes, and to distressing things that happen as I seek to do

more than survive on this planet as a woman. Beyond early traumas and the dark era of addictions, the most difficult entries document my time in India between 2001 and 2002. I live there while doing my PhD fieldwork and assist on a large international project with women and girls engaged in traditional systems of sex work. It's a fascinating opportunity but it's also stressful because I don't speak the local language, there are infrastructure issues (e.g., daily power outages, lack of telephones), and I am witness to the indignities and discrimination sex workers are subjected to, which makes me wonder if they will feel safe speaking to me. Adding insult to injury is the humiliating treatment of the women and myself by some of the academics leading the project.

Certain male team members ask the participants problematic questions about sex, health, and their bodies. They also scoff at the women's refusal to talk openly about their work and tell me to "ask them anything about sex ... it's what they do for a living." I'm instructed to remove so-called emotional details from my fieldnotes, like descriptions of my feelings and reflections on this challenging experience, and am scolded for submitting the notes late. I develop a chronic eye twitch, TMD, and skin breakouts from the stress. When I hand over my notes, what I give them is pure gold. It enriches their careers, mine too.

But they don't have a long scar that connects the skin that was closed and the future that changed direction. I never return to India as a researcher, only a tourist. This scar winds its way through every grant application, theoretical framework, and keyword I use in my research.

Postcolonial feminism. Pro–sex work feminism. Digital feminism. The scar lies flatter than it used to, but it still serves as a reminder. I run my fingers along its shiny ridge whenever I encourage my students to call out gendered injustices and to care for themselves during their research.

Those twelve months in India broke me and they made me too. They set my professional life in motion as a Kali-loving, tongue-lolling-on-the-battlefield feminist with a broader view of the world, and they convinced me, as a white, cis-gendered, able-bodied woman, of my responsibility to use my energies wisely. I don't speak for others or give people a voice, they've got their own. What I try to do is elevate, articulate, and extend the pitch of my words so that the folks at the back and the ones nestled in the ivory tower and the digital universe can hear me.

My feminist compass determines everything I do in life, including selecting a dating app. Bumble seems to be the only choice for a hopeful feminist like me. Etched in my mind is the line from Joni Mitchell's song "Same Situation" where she writes about longing for somebody who is both strong and at least somewhat sincere. Laid down in 1973 against the tapestry of her rising fame, wild Laurel Canyon parties where cocaine and quaaludes were vibing, and personal convictions, this prayer that she wrote is my prayer too.

The moment I dive into the glossy yellow Hive, I'm curious about not only the app but also its co-founder, Whitney Wolfe Herd. There must be some intriguing details about the girl boss darling who's also the youngest self-made female billionaire in history.

Bumble's Origin Story

At just thirty-four years of age, Bumble co-founder and former CEO Whitney Wolfe Herd is one of America's top female entrepreneurs, currently worth over $1.5 billion. Wikipedia tells us that she was born to a property developer and full-time mom in the Salt Lake state of Utah. Whitney goes to Southern Methodist University, where she majors in international studies. After college and volunteering abroad she helps start a not-for-profit organization to support victims of the Deepwater Horizon oil spill disaster of 2010 through the sale of cotton tote bags.

Whitney then joins Tinder in 2012 as VP of marketing, reportedly providing both the name and flame symbol for the app. She is instrumental in growing its user base, especially on college campuses, which are among the first places that Tinder is launched. Fraternities and sororities help fuel the swiping craze and provide access to marketing networks to further promote the platform.

Professional tensions and a sexual discrimination lawsuit hasten Wolfe Herd's departure from Tinder in early 2014. In September of that same year the court case is settled for over one million dollars and an undisclosed percentage of company stock. Three months later Wolfe Herd, with a few colleagues from Tinder and a sizable investment from Russian co-founder Andrey Andreev, who started the dating app giant Badoo in 2006, launches Bumble.

When thinking of a name for the platform several Russian words were pitched but they didn't stick. A board member suggested Bumble, and although Wolfe Herd wasn't into it initially, she soon harnessed the power of the queen bee symbol. In a 2015 *Esquire* interview with Natasha Zarinsky, she explains: "Bee society where there's a queen bee, the woman is in charge, and it's a really respectful community. It's all about the queen bee and everyone working together. It was very serendipitous."

Bumble is the name used for the dating platform and its BFF or "best friends forever" option, a matching system for friends. It also includes Bumble Bizz, the professional networking service, a cross between dating and LinkedIn.

According to an article on datingadvice.com published in June 2023, Bumble has over 50 million users and is the fourth-largest dating app in the world behind POF, Badoo, and Tinder. When Wolfe Herd took the company public on 10 February 2021, it was worth an estimated $8.3 billion. Bumble is a dominant force in contemporary social media and mainstream culture, and, according to a story by Clair Lui in *The Riveter*, 85 per cent of its employees are women. Approximately 50 per cent of its users are women, most of whom identify as professional, white, and under the age of thirty-five.

The story of the college volunteer becoming a global tycoon who pairs social justice with lifestyle branding on an app half the size of a postage stamp is gripping. However, there are some questionable pages in Bumble's evolution, including connections with Sophia Amaruso, whose rags-to-riches-to-bankrupt #GIRLBOSS story is one for the business vault and the tabloids. Amaruso coined term "girl-boss" after launching the wildly successful Nasty Gal clothing line in 2006, which landed her on *Forbes*'s coveted list as one of the richest self-made women in the world in 2016. Yet that same year she lost her fortune after it was revealed that working conditions at Nasty Gal were not only not fem-forward, but they were also grossly inequitable, as reported by Amanda Mull in a superb article in *The Atlantic* called "The Girl Boss Has Left the Building."

"Girl boss" used to stand for young women taking their place in the business world while not giving a damn, but now it refers to greedy and self-obsessed folks who engage in performative "wokeness." Amaruso is climbing back into the influencer ring and according to her website, she offers media marketing classes and tips for writing the perfect online bio at $1,999 a pop.

Amaruso and Wolfe Herd worked together at various social events and Amaruso's best-selling book #*GIRLBOSS* was published in 2014, the same year Bumble launched. The overlap between their brands, in particular their individualistic go-get-'em-girls-do-it-on-their-own narrative, is striking. Compare Amaruso's definition of #GIRLBOSS and Bumble's recruitment call for brand "honeys" (formerly called "ambassadors") on the Bumble lifestyle website called the BeeHive:

> A #GIRLBOSS is someone who is in charge of her own life. She gets what she wants because she works for it. As a #GIRLBOSS, you take control and accept responsibility. You're a fighter – you know when to take punches and when to roll with them. Sometimes you break the rules, sometimes you follow them, but always on your own terms. You know where you're going

but can't do it without having some fun along the way. You value honesty over perfection. You ask questions. You take your life seriously, but you don't take yourself too seriously. You're going to take over the world, and change it in the process. You're a badass. (Amaruso 2014, 11)

Bumble ambassadors make the first move. They unapologetically go after what they want. They're kind to themselves and others. They're smart, empowered individuals who want to lift others up, not push them down. Our ambassadors are leaders. They're highly involved in their communities, not hovering above them. They know they're not perfect and own that. They're Bumble team members supporting grassroots marketing, events, partnerships, local PR, community research and content creation to grow awareness for Bumble as a mission-driven platform and brand. (*The Beehive*)

It's a little confounding that Wolfe Herd continues to draw from the sinking #GIRLBOSS ship. I also find it fascinating that in this call for honeys neither feminism nor women are mentioned. How feminist is Bumble? More about this after I share what it's like to actually use the platform.

Making the First Move

I can never forget that it's my job to "make the first move" because those words are built into the template for every message I send, whether it's the first "hey" or the last "so long." Bumble is one of the only time-sensitive platforms, and I have just twenty-four hours from the time I match with someone to send the first message before the guy's account evaporates. The men to whom I send messages also have twenty-four hours to respond before they vanish "forever," to quote the fairy-tale language that's used liberally on the platform.

Intended to motivate users to keep the Hive humming, this feature doesn't always jive with my dating headspace. Spontaneity is a limited resource in my highly structured daily routine, and I usually map out my swiping activities according to my workload and where I'm at with my dating courage, or desperation. Frantic notes from the app begin appearing when there's one hour left on an initial match: "Hurry Up! You only have 1 hour left to start a chat before they disappear forever." This dramatic call to action is enhanced by the appearance of a red stopwatch around a match's picture that counts down each minute before the match expires.

Panic instead of motivation is often the end result, along with the constant reminder that the abyss of singlehood is just around the corner. The Bumble Boost package extends the time I have to make the opening line and is described as a way to help users fit dating into their busy schedules: "We know you're a Busy Bee. Extend this match for twenty-four hours and take your time." According to Bumble.com, the Boost package comes in the following tiered options: one week for $8.99, one month for $16.99, and three months for $33.99. This is a commercial pursuit as much as a romantic one.

After sending the first few messages, it dawns on me that I'm unable to access these men's accounts until they reply to me. Flipping through photos and rereading profiles is a valuable, albeit sometimes obsessive, activity to reflect on the guys who may be coming my way for dates or even just a conversation or two. Being denied access to this information seems strange and I feel like I'm powerless over my dating prospects, which is, in fact, the case.

Is this digital purgatory to protect me from thinking about a guy who might not respond? Is it to remove my ability to "bug" someone who hasn't responded? Whatever the reason, it reveals that a great deal of power is placed in the court of men, whose decision carries just as much weight as my "empowering" ability to make the first move. I wonder why this part of the journey isn't written up in the official notes on Google Play or other sites where you can download Bumble.

I thought this app was all about women being in the driver's seat? The experience feels very Orwellian, and almost like I've done something wrong. You are under review, Treena. Please stand by.

It also conflicts with the bubbly messages users get about only being as fresh as our last initial conversation and to keep that honey moving. How can we keep moving when we don't know what's going on with the guys we've contacted? Perhaps it's supposed to balance out the power we take away from men by making the first move. Maybe it's a tough love measure that helps test our resolve when men don't respond: *There there, dear, he's just not that into you. Don't make yourself sick by obsessing about it.*

Does Bumble Work?

The answer to this question depends on want you want from the app. Is it about swiping aimlessly to "see who's out there" or to stalk an ex? Maybe a FWB (friends with benefits) situation or LTR (long-term relationship) is the goal. My objectives are to meet a few guys to get busy with and develop something more lasting with one of them. Fairly straightforward, right? When the bright and speedy game begins, it feels exciting, strange, and deeply compelling. Should I swipe right more? Will that gorgeous guy respond to my opening message? Is he even real?

I'm impressed and appalled by my quick transition from a scared and confused kid with sore thumbs into a savvy digital handmaiden. I scan through screens of men at lightning speed with the Shania Twain song "I'm Gonna Getcha Good!" running through my head, especially the part where she sings with fun and confidence about all the ways she's going to get the man she wants. My opening lines get shorter, and I send more of them.

It's so fast-paced but also timeless, in the sense that there isn't an end point. How many swipes does it take for a man to appear? Shane Co., an American jeweler catering to the wedding market, polled over 1,000 dating app users with this very question. Writing for *The Loupe*, Anna Gionet reveals the eye-opening results. Using the rate of 5.83 hours of weekly swiping, the average user takes eight months and eleven days to find a partner. This works out to 3,960 individual swipes. Boomers swipe the most (6,189 times for 8.25 months), followed by Gen Xers (4,951 times for 9.5 months), millennials (3,801 times for 8.7 months), and Gen Zers (3,535 times over 5.8 months).

I find this information after exiting the Hive and so my confusion about how long it takes to achieve what I want persists for the five months that I use Bumble. During this trying and sometimes saucy time, these and other self-defeating ideas flood my skull: this is embarrassing, I can't tell anyone about this, maybe I'm too old for this, OMG – I look ridiculous in selfies, I'll never find anyone.

It's a battle between my internal pity party and knowing that the design of this platform is shaping every step of this sticky, sexy, sad situation. After all, most products in our capitalist system are manufactured to not necessarily solve problems but to create new ones that are, of course, mitigated through ever-more products and services. These tangled thoughts are hard to navigate and sometimes trust because what I'm feeling seems to be passively accepted by leagues of dating app users and writers as the new normal, subpar as it is.

Flexing my scribe muscles turns out to be a good thing, and the stats I collect (see table 1 below) about whether Bumble works or not are unique within the pantheon of dating app stories. They're very useful for three main reasons. First, numbers don't lie. People love them, have faith in them, and call them things like "evidence." I hear this frequently as a qualitative researcher whose work is often cawed at by hard science folks who live and die at the intersection of <.05 significance and describe my scholarship as "talking to people." Second, these numbers shed evidence-based light on the inconsistent return on the seemingly endless amount of labor users spend swiping on Bumble, which is often taken for granted or presumed to be exaggerated. Without this data my insights about the inequitable nature of gendered communication, and the impact of design on dating success, won't go very far. Worse, it could be interpreted as slanted hearsay. Third, this table bursts the Bumble narrative about offering easy connections that enable women to take greater control of their dating destiny.

My Bumble stats: 20 August 2017–16 January 2018

# UNIQUE MATCHES	First Moves	Replies	No Reply	Off-App Texting	Phone Calls	Men Met in Person
2,371	113	67	46	18	5	10

Only 67 of the 113 unique opening lines I create are responded to, which means that 40 per cent of my initial messages were ignored. Um, that's almost half. The rosiest story to be spun from this mess is that I have a success rate of 15 per cent (10 men met/67 responses). However, when you consider the number of men met (still 10) out of the total number of opening conversations (113) the figure is 8.8 per cent. It's even more pitiful, like less than 1 per cent, when you factor the 10 men into 2,371, which is the granddaddy total number of matches.

Although men tell me repeatedly that these results are good, if you ask me, meeting ten men in five months or two dates a month is pretty pathetic, especially when the amount of work and stress required to get those meetings is factored in. Hours and hours of texting and sexting, so many dropped conversations and ghosting. This outcome is especially abysmal compared to my primordial dating life, when I yielded a steady harvest of men for way less energy.

Unpacking why these figures are so low and what they reveal about dating, sexuality, and gender on Bumble consumes and compels me. So does the fact that nothing about my experience seems feminist. During the five months I swipe my heart out in the Hive, what yields the most attention is not my wit or fem-forward energy, it's sexualized photos. I only do this with Bumble, which is noteworthy given its status as a "feminist" dating app. I feel the need to hype up the sex to circumvent the fact that almost half of my opening lines are ignored. Isn't this ironic, and not in the Alanis sort of way?

HIM: Want to hear a joke?

ME: I do

HIM: Why did the librarian forget her books after her shift?

ME: I give up

HIM: Because she's a woman and women are stupid!

ME: Boooo. Hissss. WOW.

HIM: About 17% usually laugh

ME: Your pictures are cute but I'm not into sexism

HIM: I'm sure I don't have to tell you, but when someone tells a joke it's not serious. If you can't take that kind of comment I don't think we will get along.

ME: UNMATCH.

The Bumble Paradox

Blatant sexism like the kind displayed in this brief exchange with a Bumble match is not uncommon on dating apps. However, the fact that it happens more often on this platform, where I also engage in self-sexualization to enhance my chances of success, is compelling. The app's signature design seems to compound dating precarities and create adversarial relationships between users because everything depends on waiting. Having women make the first move may be desirable for most users, but many guys find it difficult to resolve their feelings about this power shift. Waiting to see if the men I reach out to will get back to me is kind of excruciating too, especially when so many of them don't.

Sometimes the Hive feels more like a lion's den than the sweet bee society Whitney Wolfe Herd describes it as. When the reminder messages about swiping to stay in the game pop up on my phone, I often hang my head in defeat. I'm being encouraged to get back in the ring where 40 per cent of my messages are ignored and where I get shit on regularly by rude dudes. The emphasis on my ability to succeed by swiping in what appears to be a rigged system reminds me of the cringey #GIRLBOSS lingo: "You're a fighter – you know when to take punches and when to roll with them."

These messages from Bumble also sound like diet and wellness industry mantras, which tell us to nip, tuck, and purchase smaller clothes to hang above the altars of our bathroom scales for inspiration. Never quit, never stop. These industries and #GIRLBOSS culture, both of which target women, reflect late industrial capitalism ideals about the importance of ambition, success by bootstrap pulling, and hard work to the point of suffering. But I don't sign up to Bumble to suffer. Enter what I call the "Bumble Paradox," five points that demonstrate why this platform does not deliver on its promises of being empowering and feminist:

(1) Simple messaging about feminism and equity as something women can easily obtain does not reflect our society, where sexual dynamics and gender relations are deeply contested.

(2) An app cannot achieve dating equity when widespread equity does not yet exist in society.

(3) Beyond the initial conversation, women have little control over the fate of an encounter because a match only flourishes if men respond.

(4) Removing men's profile information after women make the first move reinforces male control instead of circumventing it.

(5) The corporate narrative of quick, easy connections is misleading and discredits the tremendous labor involved in using the app, often for staggeringly low romantic returns.

Founded by a twenty-five-year-old straight, white, middle-class, cis-gender woman, Bumble's feminism reflects and is rooted in a particular socio-economic and racial location. It exemplifies what's called "popular feminism," which gives a nod to gender inequity but is primarily about individualism, marketing logic, and the power of choice. For instance, Bumble users can indicate their support for reproductive rights or gay pride in their profiles, which is then leveraged as part of their dating strategy. Bumble's uncritical deployment of the term "feminism" has many implicit and unforeseen implications for women in our patriarchal society, including the misogynistic vitriol I receive from male swipers and others who weigh in on my feminist critique of the platform.

Writing about Bumble

My first story about Bumble, called "Love, Lust and Digital Dating: Men on the Bumble Dating App Aren't Ready for the Queen Bee," is an unexpected commission. A colleague forwards me a call from an editor of an online magazine that's looking for articles about violence against Indigenous women and girls. I pitch a story about how I incorporate these sensitive issues into my university classes. The editor says that she has enough material for the Indigenous series but wonders, after perusing my website, if I can write an article about dating apps. Trepidation blends with excitement as I pull together my Bumble experiences.

That 1,100-word story opens the door to the book you are reading, and it transforms my life. In it, I describe what it's like to enter dating app land at the age of forty-five and how strange a lot of my experiences are, in and of themselves and compared to dating in analog times. I question the platform's feminist label and bemoan my meager swiping success. It's thrilling and scary to see the number of reads and shares skyrocket, hour by hour. I read and reread the article, wondering if it's even that good, while obsessively tracking the national and international publications that pick it up.

Less than twenty-four hours after its release, *The Pluralist*, a far-right journal, runs a story called: "Feminist Joins 'Empowering' Dating App – Begs for Return of Patriarchy after Constant Rejection." Full of errors and misquotes, this defamatory piece twists what I'm saying and makes me look like a complete loser. But it zips through conservative media feeds and subreddits faster than Chrissy Teigen was canceled.

Board members of the American Firearms Association even weigh in. On Twitter, American actress and proud libertarian Mindy Robinson ignites a sensational discussion with her followers.

Robinson's minions say that I deserve my dating frustrations because I'm a feminist, which means I'm unattractive, act like a man, and in all likelihood am a lesbian. Don't look now, guys, but the mid-twentieth century is in the *rear*view mirror. We let women roam on their own now. One Robinson follower comments that it looks like I comb my hair with an egg beater, which is hilarious, untrue but hilarious.

My excitement about the global uptake of the story is soon eclipsed by testy and cruel comments from readers, including the three featured in the opening to this chapter. What lights the fire of mainly male fury is my self-identified status as a feminist and the fact that I reveal my dating vulnerability as well as my sexual desire. I'm accused of "complaining" about things that men deal with all the time, namely the work involved with doing the asking out and the frustration with being rejected or ignored.

Yes, I write about these challenging things, but nowhere do I say that men don't also do a lot of dating work. I express compassion for men on Bumble because the waiting-to-be-asked-out design can make them feel excluded. Yet, this point is glossed over by every mad male reader. They're enraged when I "complain" about my meager success because apparently most men would kill for my results. That violent phrase "kill for" pops up often in the online diatribe and is reminiscent of the term "kill count" used to tally the number of sexual conquests someone has. Look at me, out there behaving like a man and not liking how it feels, boo hoo, they say.

They rail against me for being a failed man and a failed woman. In their backwater books, a woman making the first move is acting like a man and is not only unattractive to real men, but she's also disqualified from being considered a real woman. To manosphere residents, a real woman is feminine, not assertive, and lives quietly in the glass cage described at the beginning of this chapter. These male trolls are trying to taint my reputation *and* defend themselves against feminism, which they view as intrinsically prejudicial and threatening to men. They also lash out against me in an effort to affirm their sexual identity as MEN, no soft *bois* here.

At a deeper level, I think my story also provides them with a way to talk to one another about things men cannot discuss directly with each other. Things like sex, women, romantic vulnerability, and their frustration with how the shifting landscape of gender and feminism impacts them. This is reflected in the animated banter between several men in the comments section of my original article and social media spaces where my piece and *The Pluralist* story appear. Their playful conversations about ex-girlfriends, current news events, and random guy stuff sometimes take on a life of their own and after the first few jabs at me, I'm not even mentioned.

As fascinating as these observations are, being used as a digital punching bag is not fun. However, in a weird way I'm grateful for the attention because the hundreds of thousands of comments, reads, and shares on social media platforms help build my public platform as an author. Thanks, trolls!

Navigating Bumble in Real Time

With Bumble's backstory, what it's like to use the platform, and why it fails as a feminist app laid out before us, it's time to unpack what it feels like to actually use Bumble. These next sections are organized around three encounters that I call Sticky, Sexy, Sad. The first vignette features a date that went wrong and could be upsetting to anyone who has encountered sexual violence.

Sticky

Getting dressed two days later, I ruminate on how my actions could have incited his behavior. One sock, then the other, and in my mind, I hear: "I *was* sending mixed messages with the photos and saucy texts." Pulling up my underwear while looking at myself in the mirror I hear another voice that reminds me that I said "no" before anything got heavy. I *did* say no. One of the things I definitely misjudged was how invested he already was.

It starts out like all the other matches: mutual attraction, the exchange of colorful photos, and sexy textual banter. This guy is very cute and has that ripped skater look that I'll always find hot. He tells me that he was looking at my pictures for a long time before we matched, which is sort of how it works on Bumble. Guys gotta wait. But there's something about his tone that feels sketchy. I feel like I'm being watched instead of just observed as one woman in the digital dating deck. There are other red flags, like when I tell a friend that I'm not interested in having sex with this guy and that turning him down might be a challenge.

When I say we can get together, dude is over the moon. He calls me babe and sweetie, which rubs me the wrong way, but I chalk it up to extreme excitement. Why do I appease him? As dumb as it may sound, I feel like a high-roller having the attention of so many men right now. Yeah baby, get those men, win, accumulate, get those numbers. That's what the app wants me to do, right? But those numbers are people who have all sorts of illusions and desires that are impossible to truly know until you breathe the same air as them. I am also a people-pleaser and think that if I meet this guy, he'll be happy, and who knows, maybe I'll have fun too.

On the arranged day, he's running late and asks if we can connect thirty minutes later. I was fine with that but then it morphs into an hour. I sit at the bar he suggests drinking a watered-down ginger ale with a dry lime wedge, growing less enchanted as the minutes pass. He finally shows up and he says repeatedly that he adores me. How is that possible, when all he has to go on are photos and a few texts? He's also told a lot of his friends about me and seems surprised that I haven't done the same. "You're exactly what I like ... we won't tell people we met on Bumble." We?

He reaches across the table and takes my hand in his shaky palm. I look at him while he searches my face for clues about what might happen. From the waitress's sideways glance, I know that my ICK feelings are shining through. I free myself from his awkward grasp and then we're crossing the street to go to his place, which is a couple of minutes away. I debate sprinting away, but that seems harder or registers as more dangerous than going along with things. Maybe if I give him a little, he'll leave me alone.

We kiss on his bed in the cramped, dark bedroom and I feel myself retreating from what's happening. He tugs more than once at my jeans, and I pull away from him and tell him that I'm not taking my pants off or having sex. I do not want to be here and go through the motions while feeling insecure, and increasingly scared. When I say no a second time (or is it a third?) and get off the bed, he quickly bounds up after me and blocks the bedroom door. His face suddenly looks scary and unattractive.

While untangling my escape options, electric surges of panic run through my body. Despite all the information coursing through me, I can't think or move. It lasts only seconds, but those seconds feel achingly long. "You're freaking me out," I say while backing away from him. He looks at me, wide-eyed, and reaches at my body again. I say it again: "NO, you're freaking me out right now." He stops and I see my bag just outside his bedroom door, a beacon of security and where my phone is. I grab my top, stumble into the bathroom, and quickly lock the door.

It's boiling inside and I pray that he won't be waiting for me when I open it. He's not. After I leave the bathroom he pulls me back into his bedroom and says "Let's talk," while inching closer to me. I pull away: "Sorry, I don't feel okay." "Seriously? Come on Treena. I like you so much," he pleads in disbelief and frustration. I move towards the building foyer and turn back to look at him. "Sweetheart, I need to take care of myself," I say, still performing for him on the edge of freedom.

I barge out the door into the half-lit afternoon of early winter and take a deep breath of cold air. I made it out, I'm okay. I keep moving but have no idea where I'm going. I feel like people are looking at me with concern. My face is not a mask but a mirror of what just happened. I select some music and hope he's not following me. The Clash, that's what I'll listen to. I can feel tough and cool in their rock-ska beats. Protect me. I debate calling friends but don't want to open up or come undone, not yet. "I'm okay," I keep saying this to myself, which is true, but I'm also completely traumatized.

I make it to a familiar downtown hotel and plop myself down on one of the plush couches in the lobby. People mill around me, smartly dressed bellhops wait on customers, and there is a feeling of being hidden in plain sight. I see his text and answer it with trembling hands. I don't respond to his apology and provide my home address instead. I forgot my beautiful Max Mara sunglasses and want them back, desperately.

When I tell people this later their jaws drop because I've just shared the details of where I live. Pure recovery mode will do this to people. The next day I buy myself a new pair at the Sunglass Hut at the Eaton Centre. How symbolic, to exchange one way of looking at the world and my experiences for another. To see differently.

I glance around the hotel lobby and begin studying the people around me, which is grounding. It reminds me of the 5-4-3-2-1 exercise I do with my counselor. The one where you name five things you can see, four things you can feel, three things you can hear, two things you can smell, and one thing you can taste. The meanings of this day shape-shift across space and time as I process it and find somewhere to lay it away. This experience I didn't expect to have; these memories I don't want.

Sexy

The G-string I plop into my purse jostles around with the travel size tube of Astroglide and a hand towel, which seems like a suitable accessory for a tryst with him. He's around 6'4", very well-built, and from Quebec. A play on poutine, the famous Quebec meal of french fries, cheese curds, and gravy, my friends call him "Mantine." He is good enough to eat and this is the third twenty-dollar Uber ride I've taken to his hotel room in the last two months.

It's the same hotel where I attend dreary work retreats and is located on a dead stretch of a main thoroughfare dotted with big box stores, a Red Lobster restaurant, and several Korean nail salons. The smell of chlorine from the pool wafts towards me as I wait for the double glass doors to slide open.

Stepping into the hotel feels transgressive. It's nighttime and I've only been here during the day. I'm here for sexy times and not work. I'm also in commando mode, which I almost never do in general and certainly never at work. No shade to folks who do. I nod to the middle-aged guy behind the desk, who looks bored and a little sad in his ill-fitting suit. It's empty and as I walk the quiet carpeted corridors, I feel sneaky and a bit impish. I laugh at the terrible hotel art and wonder what's in store for *ce soir*. With Kendrick Lamar's song "Humble" in my ears, I silently do the chicken and purse my lips to the lines about stretch marks and being tired of photoshop.

I check my phone again for the room number and knock on the door. Nothing. I gasp when I realize it's the wrong one – OMFG. I blast down the hall and after catching my breath, I find the right room. The door's been left ajar, and I slowly push it open. I hear the shower running and see a mist of steam gathering on the mirror next to the bathroom. With my right index finger, I make the imprint of a happy face and begin to get undressed.

He's the first guy on Bumble to cut to the chase and ask me, "What do you want on here?" I'm heading into a second-hand bookstore to find a copy of *White Teeth* by Zadie Smith when this message comes shooting into my hand. Instead of the usual idle chatter and generic sexual banter that feels pretty meaningless with a stranger, he wants to know what I'm looking for to determine if chatting is worth our time. Respect. "Something casual but I'm open to more," I reply, and he sends three kissing face emojis that tell me we're on the same page.

Although I provide this exact information in my profile, I'm not too annoyed at repeating myself because at this early stage of my Bumble journey it's refreshing to be asked for confirmation. However, over time this question drives me nuts because virtually every guy asks me what I'm looking for. I'VE WRITTEN IT OUT FOR YOU!!! This query reflects how little attention people pay to the profiles and it also reveals the deep-rooted assumption among users that everyone's profiles are bunk or that we're all trying to deceive one another.

When I meet Mantine, I like him immediately because he seems confident but also quiet, and he's incredibly sexy. When we're in bed, it's hot and fun. He's as big as a continent and I love crawling all over and around him. After scaling his landscape, we have several poignant exchanges about dating, popular culture, and relationships. He tells me that he feels "useless" as a man, referring to the fact that women don't need men for jobs, providing the basics of life, or even having kids. I mention love and sex and emotional connection as things a lot of women want and need. He says that most women he interacts with on Bumble are after men with perfectly sculpted bodies who can offer them luxe lifestyles.

I wonder if that's what these women are after or if they're just parroting what's sold online as the things to aspire to. The shallowness makes me shudder and, whether it's what these women want or not, it's what they tell him. No wonder he feels hopeless. It's good to be able to burst that bubble a bit with some wisdom from an older woman who's lived a lot before anything digital came along and who's interested in how men think about the shifting sands of gender, sex, and power. He tells me after each date how much he appreciates being able to talk about this stuff with someone who cares. Gulp. Men need to feel supported and safe to share themselves more.

When I inquire about his assessment of Bumble, he's not shocked by the things I find bewildering – the work, the bullshit responses, the no responses, the speed with which people indicate their interest and then disappear. He's ten years younger than me and far more experienced in the realm of digital culture. Mantine also has way less analog dating years under his belt and so this "new normal" is quite normal to him. Although the dates continue to be fun, he gets soft more often and the thrill tapers away on my end too. Over the next few weeks our communication stops, no games or meanness, just goodbye.

Sad

After texting for a while, this guy shares a photo that stops me in my tracks. He stands shirtless in the middle of an untidy, sparsely decorated bedroom. I observe pudginess and a very "unique" tattoo. Is that a lacrosse stick or a baton? Several different items are jammed together in a small area of his chest, it looks kinda random. His sandy hair is styled in an outdated Justin Bieber swoop. He looks lonely and vulnerable, and yet it takes courage to send me this picture. There's a lot going on and it feels both unsettling and interesting.

Despite having little sexual interest in this person, I continue to answer his texts and plan a date. I'm sort of embarrassed to acquiesce to this guy, but then maybe I can provide some sexual healing. Cue Marvin Gaye's brilliant lyrics about the miraculous powers of sex, which can stave off blue teardrops and the seas that storm inside us when we're not getting that connection and release we all need. I'm not going to whisper "get up, get up, get up, get up" into this guy's ear, but part of me feels a sense of humanitarianism in being able to provide him something that he doesn't get too often.

Is this the antithesis of being a feminist or is it precisely what it's about – caring for others? Where am I in this equation – a silly siren of unpaid sexual service? A politically motivated passion provider?

When I share my mixed feelings about this guy with my friends, most of them support the date. You might enjoy yourself, they say. One woman describes his picture as "normal," the kind of guy you can have coffee with and not feel the need to talk. I'm looking for fun, not to be someone's quiet counsel! I want to carve out a new sexual path that is more about me and my sexual pleasure than it is about appeasing the men I encounter, but it's hard to shift gears and put my desires into action.

Standing up for the sexual empowerment of others is far easier than doing it in my own life. Doing it for myself means believing that I'm worth more than I've been socialized as a woman to accept. How can I tell if what I think is feminist isn't just another version of losing myself in the sea of male oppression?

I share my predicament with a former friend, who hisses at me in rage for calling myself a feminist. She speaks of my behavior in the same breath as male violence against women and accuses me of promoting this community service approach to sex. She also indicates that I'm a terrible role model for young women. OUCH. I'm just sharing my experiences and certainly not telling anyone to do as I do. I don't think that every sexual encounter necessarily needs be sacred or about love. Perhaps she does.

As he lumbers towards the back door of my building, I peer through the curls of decorative metal that lay behind the glass squares on the top portion of the back door. EGADZ!! He's a country boy in a red and black checkered Western jacket. He seems drained of vital energies and has the mannerisms of someone twice his age of thirty years. His quiet motions of passion scarcely register a sound and yet the smile that never leaves his face after a certain point feels a bit gratifying.

I wish him a safe drive home and say it was nice to meet him, which isn't entirely true but it's not entirely false either. He wants to meet again but I don't and say, "We'll see." I avoid further communication by using the protective wreath of Christmas travel to family far away as an excuse. I accomplish my goal of doing him a favor, so I think, but it feels very empty. I feel empty and don't want to be asked for more. He's likely pretty confused and maybe hurt.

There are a few more awkward requests on his end that likely feel as grim to receive as they are to send. No more charity, which is a thorny – not horny – pursuit that fuels longing among those in need and sets in motion fruitless pursuits for those with misplaced goods to give.

Feminish Revisited

I download Bumble to help alleviate my anxiety about getting back in the romance game and hope it aligns with some of my feminist ideals. But the lifestyle-driven feminism and problematic design thwart both of these aims on a consistent basis. Ultimately, Bumble is a place of waiting. Women go first and wait for men to respond. Men wait to be asked and although they are denied the dating power they're used to (i.e., going first or at least at the same time as women), they have the upper hand in other ways because their response determines the fate of a match.

The question about whether or not Bumble delivers on its promises of a dating revolution is paramount to understanding my experiences, which I find hard to organize emotionally and intellectually. *Is* it feminist? Am *I* feminist when I hypersexualize myself to increase my chances of getting male attention? Lolling around in my mind with these questions is the image of Vicky Pollard, a character in the brilliant British TV series *Little Britain*. Known for wearing tight pink tracksuits, sporting dated blonde hair with sausage roll bangs, and having questionable boyfriends, her famous line "Ya but, no but" feels entirely accurate.

These questions stick with me because selling this easy-breezy feminism in a world that's still hostile to women feels irresponsible. The individual-oriented empowerment in a bubble message is the clickbait; it obscures what lurks beneath, the #GIRLBOSS feminism designed to hook users in the swiping game and make money instead of creating equitable relationships. I think back to Wolfe Herd's account of honeybee society as "respectful ... everyone working together," which couldn't be further from the truth. Bee colonies are among the most hierarchically structured animal communities; the workers literally die for their queen and the upkeep of the hive.

Despite the bubblegum version of feminism on the dating app, Wolfe Herd has initiated some positive and empowering moves that can help improve women's lives. This includes initiatives like outlawing unsolicited dick pics on Bumble and taking out full-page advertisements in the *Wall Street Journal* and *New York Times* that say "Believe Women" during the Kavanaugh investigation in 2018. I support these feminist acts, but because dick pics rarely come my way on the app, they don't really impact my swiping life on Bumble or make it any easier to navigate the misogyny that feels extra rampant on the app.

If we can create 3D printers that make customized medical implants to save people's lives, surely we can design a sexy, fem-forward dating app that includes guys and other gendered folks in cool ways. The question is: Why haven't we? Something else we need is a better way of talking to men about what it's like to be a woman. This includes the guys in the manosphere like those who responded wildly to my first Bumble article; they reveal the inky underbelly of modern manhood and the threatened state of feminism. One minute I laugh about it and the next I delete another email from another angry man.

My experiences inside the Hive also illuminate how hard it can be for women to say no to men in all sorts of dating situations. For many of us, even street-smart feminists like me, it often feels easier or less threatening to put ourselves in harm's way than it is to use the letters N – O. Saying no shouldn't be so mind-bendingly difficult and yet it is. It's not simply or only my fault when I get tangled up in that basement apartment with a man who no longer looks like a man through the lens of terror. I'm afraid to say no because I'm worried about the prospect of violence. I also don't want to hurt his feelings, which I privilege over my own safety because women are socialized to be service providers to men, to not disappoint them, to not make them mad.

That man doesn't outright ask to be serviced, but it's implied in the systems of power through which he operates. It's reflected in him putting constant pressure on me to do something I said I didn't want to do and his shock at me wanting to leave his apartment. "But I like you so much," he keeps saying, as if that should keep me there. My terror is invisible and less important than his desire. When the prospect of protecting myself from a man is more difficult than acquiescing to him, what surfaces, among other things, is how limited women's power can be and how difficult this makes navigating not only sex and gender, but also basic communication.

This happens to me at the age of forty-five, not twenty-five, and it happens with someone I meet on a feminist app that we both signed up for.

Saying no is hard even when men aren't dangerous. This truth rings loud in my ears when I think about the sad guy. Why don't I just say no to a date with him? Is my benevolence a veil for something far less admirable, patronizing even? Saying no to men still feels mean despite all the social narratives about being honest and taking care of number one. How absurd to think that not doing what other people want is mean – to think this is to step back into the fog and disappear myself. It can be so hard to see myself sometimes.

Elissa Bassist devotes a chapter of her book *Hysterical: A Memoir* to the problem of women not saying no, which she writes about eloquently:

> "No" expires at the back of women's throats on purpose. The disease to please is our birth defect, and then we're brought up to be obliging, reassuring, and noncombative. To refuse is "demanding," "hostile," and "hideous," and we should not hurt someone else's feelings by expressing our own. (Bassist 2023, 95)

Closing Thoughts: Laying Pipe

"You say you're a feminist ... Why do they make such a big deal out of it?" asks Mike the plumber a couple of weeks ago. Jolts of excitement and worry streak through me. I tell him that I'm so glad he asked me this and that I've just been writing about it. Would he like to hear some of chapter 3 of my book? After he nods, I grab the laptop and plop myself down on the bathroom floor, where he's scraping old caulking off the bottom of my sink with a utility knife.

I think that it'll be a slam dunk to show him how righteous the feminist battle is when I mention rates of intimate partner violence and femicide. I flatten the fingers of my right hand and pull them across the air to make an imaginary flat line as I tell Mike that these rates have remained steady for decades despite the gains we have made. I throw my head back and shake it from side to side when saying "all the gains" we've made. Perhaps by dramatizing these things I have a better chance of helping him understand why feminists make a big deal. He doesn't nod like I anticipated; he just quietly looks at me. What does Mike hear when I say these things?

I jostle my legs under the laptop and smile while saying that he's the first person to hear this part of the chapter. The show must go on. I read four paragraphs and try to gauge his response as he lowers the braided steel facet connectors into the base of the pedestal sink. When Mike chuckles at the "littlest feminist on the prairie" part I breathe a sigh of relief and we both laugh. He asks about the word "liberal," which I mention when describing different kinds of feminists.

Then the plumber shares his own stories about a painful custody battle and jarring events from his days in the military when some of the male members of the platoon would catcall and sexualize the women soldiers horribly. Mike searches his life for something to show me that he gets what I'm trying to do. I scroll through my phone to stem the tears that are forming and secretly bask in what feels like a standing ovation.

A few minutes later we gather downstairs while Mike cleans up, and he asks what I teach at the university. I tell him, "I teach about the topics I do research on, things like sexuality, gender, and health. Also dating apps." When I tell Mike this he leans in my direction and says, "I hate dating apps!" I've been granted two golden eggs on this day of clogged pipes, first the inquiry about feminism and now this. I smile in disbelief when he tells me, sheepishly with a sideways grin, that he's only used Bumble.

He doesn't call it feminist but likes when women ask him out and adds, "It's supposed to have better looking girls too, more professional." I signed up for the exact same reasons, but for guys.

As he scours the last of the grit off his hands at my kitchen sink, I ask how it's going on Bumble. He shakes his head and tells me that women typically say "hi" and then they disappear or expect him to carry the conversation. Being "hi'd," as I call it. Have I done it? YES, but only two or three times to see what would happen. Spoiler: Nothing happens when all you give is two letters.

Mike also says that some of his matches have "mental health issues," but I'm not sure what that means exactly. Are these women as mad as everyone around the tea table in Wonderland? Do confusing and inconsistent equal mental health issues? Or do the apps drive his matches batty, as batty as they've driven me and many men I've encountered in Swipedom?

Mike's gonna ditch Bumble and go old school, like "going to the grocery store five times a week." "I need more eeegplaants!!" I say and we both laugh. Before he exits the Hive he's game for me to give his profile a peek-a-view. He hands me his phone, which is a gesture of trust, and it also signals his genuine desire to connect with someone. I feel like a digital soothsayer, reading his profile like a fortune teller would read a palm. My secret eye, the thing that allows me to see what he cannot, however, is not a special occult power passed down across the centuries by a witch or a prophetess. It is my gender. I use this slit in my body to reveal sacred information that could help him in his quest for romance and possibly change the trajectory of his life.

First, I advise him to indicate what he's looking for in his profile. If you're interested in something meaningful and monogamous put it out there. If short-term and casual is your thing, put it down. Second, I tell him to lose one of the three rock climbing pictures, the one where the angle is strange and makes him look like Gumby plastered against a Sedona cliff. Third, can we lose or edit the opening quote? No dice. When Mike asks if I know where it's from, I realize it's famous.

I have no clue and scream when he says: *"Ferris Bueller's Day Off."* Such a classic 1980s film! When I think of this movie, the lines "Bueller ... Bueller ..." come to mind but not this quote, which seems a very apropos place to conclude this journey through the feminish forest: "The question isn't, 'what are we going to do?' The question is, 'what aren't we going to do?'"

This lovely exchange between strangers feels organic and so different from the many encounters on Bumble and other apps, where the design of the algorithm as well as the way the platforms are marketed exerts tremendous influence. This is what awaits us in chapter 4 and, trust me, although it's called "Copy & Paste" there's nothing generic about it.

FOUR

Copy & Paste

Beyond the huge volume of people to scroll through, the main difference between swipe culture and my rock-and-roll analog days is independence. Previously I was a free agent, not so with dating apps because I'm routinely managed and coached by people at Dating App Head Quarters. Those folks who issue punchy messages about swiping more and getting out there. Don't leave that match waiting. Listen b*tch, I'm paying for this so can you leave me alone. Actually, I'd like some help to make this experience a lot more interesting and can do without the corporate mumbo jumbo.

How many millions of other users receive those same messages? What do they think of them? So many things about this experience feel carbon copy, including the nearly identical conversations I have with my friends about their dating lives. There are also the texts I have with men of all ages, most of whom say pretty much the same things and then often go "poof." Flirting has always been the super fun stage of getting to know someone, but now it's sort of hollow. Are these men all the same? Do they find our exchanges boring? Maybe that's why they ghost so often.

Being stuck inside this monotonous cycle makes me question whether random things can still happen. I practice my "hello, stranger" skills with a cute guy who works at the market. What if I fell in love with him while paying for some radishes? Would it work? Would he be repelled or, God help me, unable to recognize what I'm doing? Do people find themselves in the lives of someone totally new at the drop of a hat or a vegetable anymore? I like to think so, but do we have the courage to risk an unscripted encounter?

All of this makes me retreat until there's just a listless thumb hanging outside of my shell. It's wet and shimmery inside but few men will ever see the silver rainbow reflected on the ceiling. Perhaps all I can give and receive is a kind of half-love, which is about as much as anyone puts out on dating apps. That so many of us are willing to sit under a plastic sky of maybe, hoping that our arrows will land is quite incredible. Can digital lovers ever be "star-crossed"?

We give ourselves away on swiping platforms because we don't trust one another to do the human work of communicating and meeting in the flesh. The practice of talking on phones is nearly extinct because, apparently, it's too stressful. FFS. Maybe there are other reasons that make dating apps feel impossible and boring, things that are hidden from us by the metal hearts that manufacture our dependence on devices that are fundamentally about the sixteen digits on a credit card. That's the swipe at the center of swipe culture, not romance.

Dating apps are flattening out the variability in our relationships, they're diluting the diversity in our intimate experiences. I recoil in horror when a student tells me that her dating encounters are "identical" to mine. My sex life isn't supposed to be identical to someone who's two decades younger than me, and this certainly wasn't the case until dating went digital. In the before times, my romantic pursuits were wild, fun, and sometimes a bit dark, but they were certainly unique to me. Now, it's copy and paste.

As a fervent Sagittarian born under the patchouli skies of the 1970s, I love diversity in all its forms. It's a fundamental principle in anthropology too, a discipline that is founded on knowing ourselves in relation to how other people live and think about the world. During my PhD fieldwork in India, for instance, countless people said they felt sorry for me because I have to find a partner on my own. Through their lens, arranged marriages are better because they involve a team of family members, religious folks, and astrologers to chart out the most suitable match.

Initially, I think, "Oh Ganesh, where is the autonomy in that, and what about love?" However, in cultures where the relationship between the individual and society is more important than the individual alone, marriage functions more to join families and continue the kin line than to fulfill romantic dreams. My Indian friends also point to the fact that so many Westerners get divorced as evidence that our approach has some glitches. Touché. They're different cultural solutions to the universal quest for sex, love, and the continuation of our species.

Beyond my experiences, I learn a great deal about swipe culture from listening to how other people survive and periodically thrive on "the apps." Sometimes new insights flicker into view by chance, like on that September afternoon. Thick strokes of sunlight fall across the surface of my desk, where I'm seated next to one of my students. After discussing an upcoming assignment, I begin wailing about my atrocious dating app encounters. Instead of being wide-eyed and shocked, she takes in my information with the ease of someone sipping a glass of water.

I want her to be outraged and agree that I'm being treated abominably. But instead, she very coolly says, "Treena, your experiences are identical to ours. You seem so upset about this." While shaking my head side to side in bewilderment, I exclaim, "Yes, and you don't. That seems like a problem to me." All of this is just another day in Swipedom for her. A sense of melancholy washes over me when I realize that the empty and often infuriating swiping system may be all this young woman will ever know about dating and sex.

I don't necessarily want her to be rolling around the rural hills of Appalachia taking Percocets with a gorgeous, unstable man she met during a boozy conference weekend. Nor do I think it's a fantastic idea for her to have a failed threesome with some high school friends. However, the exploration and thrills that form the bedrock of my pre-app dating life provide a distinctly unique and invaluable education. Through these encounters I learn a great deal about power and human vulnerability, and how to nurture my sexual capital.

My intrepid romantic life is threatened by the generic experiences created on dating apps. Is all the fun, exhilaration, and unpredictability eroded when we rely on swiping? If the variability and wildness is rooted out, then what's left over? I tug on the strings of my thinking cap to make sense of this. The voice of famed media analyst Marshall McLuhan, which I imagine to be low and deadpan in that 1960s news documentary way, looms in my head. The medium is the message. Isn't that a bit deterministic?

Let's unpack how this flattening out of diversity works. I'm especially interested in who is directing this process and how it might be impacting us on a global scale for reasons that extend beyond the ups and downs of dating relationships. Also, why do we settle for dating experiences that are so similar and so lame, what I refer to as "meh"?

Making Sense of "Meh"

At the outset of my swiping odyssey, I interpret the huge piles of confusion, failure, and replica encounters exactly how the dating app industry wants me to. I blame myself. I'm just an old luddite. I'm not that hot. I don't spend enough time on the apps. Well, those self-deprecation days are over and I'm diving into the anatomy of dating apps to figure the "meh" out. Never has boring sounded so fascinating, right?

Dating app design and algorithms play central roles in the production of "meh." They rely on the principle of operant conditioning, which is a defining characteristic of most dating platforms. Like slot machines and other reward-driven products, swipers are hooked by scoring intermittent wins amid loses. Insert image of elderly woman tethered to a slot machine in Reno. I'm not that far off as I chant "mama needs some new shoes" while waiting for hot guys to appear in my roster, which happens with calculated infrequency. It drives me mad, and it keeps me swiping.

As Dan Slater explains in his book *Love in the Time of Algorithms*, a happy customer is bad for the dating app business. Failure is bred into the circuitry of dating apps and user experiences. Remember, it isn't all about you.

Not that we are mindless zombies who exert zero influence over our romantic lives. The point is that the dating app labyrinth is designed to offer few options for us; we are unlikely to get lost or to take random detours of our own choosing. There'll be no heroic Sir Didymus leading us past the Bog of Eternal Stench towards a path of sexy delights. This takes a while to sink in because, frankly, it's a bit depressing to realize that corporate motives are directly influencing my sexual-love-lust life. I want it to remain wild, sacred, and mine. I don't want it to be a product.

The way we use products like services also contributes to "meh." This is called servitization and a good example is how we can't buy Adobe Acrobat, but we can rent it to make PDFs and fill in those forms that never work. People download Tinder and use it as a dating and social networking service. Without social instruction beyond simplistic dos and don'ts, dating apps aren't a service; nor do they teach us anything about dating. As Helen Fisher, resident scientist at Match.com, says in a 2019 article by Emily Reynolds in *The Guardian*: "This is new technology and nobody has ever told us how to use it. They're not dating sites, they're introducing sites."

"Meh" is also directly shaped by the concept of McDonaldization: yes, this is a real term. Developed in the early 1990s by American sociologist George Ritzer, it refers to the particular way we think about production, work, and consumption in the late twentieth century. Basically, the idea is that these elements of our global economy are developed to mirror the characteristics of a fast-food restaurant – efficiency, calculability, predictability, standardization, and control. Adapting these principles to our society creates massive ripple effects and one of them is the homogenization or uniformity of economic and social life. Sound familiar?

These insights about how apps work and what we're doing when we use them contradict social media narratives about easy, breezy connections being just a swipe away. Yet, they also feed into deep-rooted cultural ideas about working hard at things that are important to us.

We're socialized to believe that struggle is an essential component of meaningful life events. It makes victories sweeter, is a badge of honor, and is reflected in how we valorize both work and sacrifice. Think of terms like "labor of love" or phrases like "it's not work if you love your job" and "true success requires sacrifice." These beliefs are mobilized by the dating industry when, while stacking the deck, it positions swiping as a fun and special game worth playing. They must find ways for us to keep swiping and clicking on the advertisements selectively placed throughout the interface.

When these sneaky design issues are considered alongside the oft-repeated mantra that digital dating is the "only" way to meet people, it's no wonder most of us plod away in misery. Or we delete the apps when we can't stand it anymore and then reinstall them months, days, or sometimes hours later. According to Jasmin Jones, culture editor at *The Arrow*, the skewed ratio between suffering and success is why we, and by we I mean over 90 per cent of dating app users, do the uninstall and reinstall dance.

In his book about the politics of dating apps in urban China, Lik Sam Chan discusses at length the cycle of uninstalling and reinstalling dating apps. Shani Silver talks about it too in *A Single Revolution*, where she issues a bold call to action to end the un/reinstall dance. Basically, she says, "Delete Your Dating Apps," which is also the title of one of her book chapters. An article by Jenn Kirsch in the *Toronto Star* describes a similar move among single women in their early twenties to late forties living in Toronto, which is similar to New York City in terms of its dating challenges. Many women interviewed are deleting their dating apps because, except for frustration, they have nothing to show for their years of swiping.

Interestingly, Kirsch notes that their dating app experiences are "almost copy-and-paste similar." This doesn't make the challenges associated with swiping any less awful to go through, but it contextualizes them in a way that reveals the limited influence we have over our online fails and successes. The multiple ways the dating industry infiltrates our swiping behaviors and how we make sense of their products also reduces the likelihood that we will look to the apps as the source of our hair-tearing frustration. After all, we get some wins every now and then, and if we're all having the same experiences, the frustration and periodic agony must be on us, right?

Here are some examples of how these platforms dilute the variability of our sexual and romantic lives, which I call the ten faces of "meh":

1. Recycling: When men I swipe left on keep coming back into my swipehouse like a discarded boomerang. I keep swiping left and they keep swiping right, or are they swiping left on me too? We're both being flipped by an algorithm that wants to reshuffle our lives in a particular way. It doesn't give up and neither should we, is that

the idea? I know it's not personal, but it makes me feel like my "no" is meaningless and that feels crappy, especially when I pay for Gold or VIP packages.

2. El Boro: Most dating apps are pretty boring to use. We move our thumbs in one or two directions and spend most of our time culling through unkempt or weird profiles. A cap is placed over the natural steam, the innate whir of the body and the mind that happens when you fall for someone. This unfun play of the game reduces us to generic players and empties the fun out of things really fast.

3. Schmoozing: I often feel reduced to garden variety back-and-forths to impress, repel, and sometimes manipulate men. This repetitive work, with the faintest glimmer of enticing possibility, sums up most of my time on dating apps. It's like we are acting and testing one another. There's no secret pattern or ticket to winning, and almost everyone moves on in a heartbeat. Why do I keep asking how their night was?

4. Copy & paste: I have identical conversations with hundreds of men. I only copy and paste the same message from one inbox to another a couple of times, but a lot of people do it a lot. It's linked with objectification, laziness, and the volume of people we move through on the regular. There's also the fact that most of us duck out sooner or later, so why do original dialogue? It's certainly appreciated but can be an unwise investment of energies in the long run.

5. The modern trinity: Work, gym, and school form the baseline of most male dating app user profiles and

pics. They don't all go to the gym, but say they do because it's cool and we're supposed to. Additional "everyman" activities like travel, coffee, good food, movies, music, hanging out, and having fun are mentioned so often that many profiles could be switched out for one another. It makes me wonder what's special about these men as individuals.

6. Call of dating: The gamification of dating transforms the pursuit of romance into a leisure activity. According to *Forbes* writer Theo Miller, this aspect of swiping can "flatten the users' thought processes once the real-life dating occurs, turning it into a situation wherein the right responses trigger a certain point value." Being reduced to a point value is awful and it can hasten the dehumanizing treatment of one another on and off the screen.

7. Bro-tox: The dating app industry is driven by cis-hetero masculine desires, including toxic bro culture. As Nancy Jo Sales says, in a 2021 *Slate* article, "Dating apps did not invent misogyny, but they weaponized it." This is reflected in the lack of safety protocols on most apps, despite piles of research demonstrating the links between dating apps and violence, especially towards women.

8. So tired: Using dating apps requires loads of time and emotional and sexual labor. Many users scroll for around ninety minutes a day, which is the equivalent of three episodes of *Fleabag*. There are only twelve episodes of this brilliant show, and you don't want to watch this many in a day because the withdrawals will be swift. Pace yourself. It's the same for dating apps, which can be exhausting and demoralizing.

9. Dating creep: Most social media platforms have direct messaging features that people use to gain sexual access to one another. Sliding into someone's DMs is part of our cultural lexicon about modern romance. In 2021, *Cosmo* ran a story about it and there are countless song references, memes too. Unwanted messages like, "Hello, can I be your sugar daddy?" "You're so beautiful, like an angel," and "I'm a hard-working Christian man looking for a wife" are irritating to receive and they remind me how few spaces in this world are free from male invasion.

10. Sex hub: The pornification of dating app dialogues flattens our erotic imagination. I'm struck by the indistinguishable nature of so many men's sexts, which usually read like an instruction manual: "I'll do this" and "You'll do this." When I disrupt these yawn-inducing scripts and say, "let's see how it goes when we meet," I'm met with: "heh heh … you're gonna do …" These men are creating a story for their own purposes and pleasure, and I'm just a character who comes out when needed. I could be anyone.

How "Meh" Is Made

After fleshing out how "meh" shows up on swiping platforms, I want to dig a bit deeper into the higher-level factors at play. First up is the way that dating app companies present their products, especially the algorithms. I'll focus on Tinder and Bumble because I use them extensively, and they're among the most powerful players in the industry in terms of user numbers, marketing muscle, and cultural influence. Hinge also gets some love towards the end.

Tinder

Every time I cruise this website, I'm seduced by its slick look, chill-vibing verbiage, and the slightly naughty feel of that trademark red. According to schemecolor.com, the color of the Tinder app icon is an exclusive blend of Electric Pink, Fiery Rose, and Pastel Red.

The Tinder Tech Blog is a bonanza of insider articles about the industry and top company influencers, including Chief Technology Officer Tom Jacques, described as "leading the charge of improving dating technology for the greater good." As a "veteran in online dating science," he "works with his team to solve technical challenges, eliminate fraud and bad actors, and architect high-performing technology." Tinder's use of war, science, and social justice lingo to describe a tech position is fascinating.

It's effective too. This rock-solid, progressive, future-looking framing of their man in charge generates consumer trust in Tom and, by extension, the app itself. How can you *not* have confidence in Tom? It also reduces the likelihood that users will question the app's design when or if they run into snags. The Pressroom page is where the company sheds light on its secret sauce, the Rosetta Stone of dating apps, the algorithm:

> We're happy to share more details behind how the Tinder algo-
> rithm works. Allow us to blow your minds. The most important

factor that can help our members improve their match potential on Tinder is ... using the app.

But it's not only about swiping all the time because on another page Tinder says we should swipe at the same time as like-minded people. Who dat? Like-minded peeps are determined by shared interests, similar photos, and the same likes and dislikes. It's being similar that counts. Yet, the slogan "swipe right on diversity" also appears on the website, alongside this bold statement: "Our algorithm doesn't track social status, religion or ethnicity. We don't believe in stereotypes ... Our algorithm is designed to be open and we love the results."

How can similarity and diversity both be tracked on the algorithm? Is the latter an attempt to appear inclusive and attentive to equity-related issues? Maybe it's to broaden their current demographic, which seems to be reflected in the "everything-to-everybody" product description:

> There really is something for everyone on Tinder. Want to get into a relationship? You got it. Tinder is where adults of all backgrounds and experiences are invited to make connections, memories, and everything in between. New kid on campus and looking to make the most of your college experience? Tinder U's got you covered.

Tinder U, who knew? I won't apply to work there just yet though because it seems like a kappa beta data harvesting class. Users are asked to provide their ".edu email address" and after verifying a few things they're "In Tinder U! Swipe, match, and message as usual – you know the curriculum – it's Tinder 101." The "101" and "blow your minds" comments verge on condescending. Like, dude, it's so basic. Duh. Elsewhere swiping success is described as being "totally in our members' control," which reinforces the incorrect notion that users are solely responsible for their dating app results.

Bumble

It's always sunny on Bumble with that buttery yellow gleaming through every swipe and product placement. Both yellow *and* white are trademark colors of this brand, which, according to brandpalettes.com, "represents good times and simplicity." Unlike Tinder's one-swipe-fits-all – just-use-the-frickin'-app – approach, Bumble is more overtly tailored towards women and dating equity. Bumble is very hush-hush about the algorithm, but a few tech-savvy folks on Reddit and other online spaces have some ideas about how the "women go first" platform works.

One of them is the "Elo rating system," which is used to calculate players' skill levels in zero-sum games where there is one winner and one loser (e.g., poker, gambling, chess). The relative skill level in this instance refers to how appealing someone's profile is, which is based on appearance, career type, and personality. Given the small space allotted to the written portion of the profile where users can express their personality (300 characters with spaces), the first two factors are the heavy hitters.

It's impossible to know if the company uses the Elo system, but Bumble users I've spoken with consistently say that looks are most important and it's a hard app to master if people don't swipe right on you enough, which is the equivalent of being rated as not "hot." The superficial nature of this platform is reflected in a hilarious 2018 r/Bumble Reddit post entitled "I only see hot people." Apparently conventionally beautiful people are rewarded more often than regs like us: unsettling, especially on an app that's marketed as modern and feminist.

Despite the "pretty people only" reputation, Bumble prides itself on promoting kindness, safety, and empower-ment, as reflected on their website: "We prioritize kindness and respect, providing a safe online community for users to build new relationships. Bumble empowers users to connect with confidence." The site displays equity-friendly "success stories" to validate this claim, featuring couples of various races, sexual orientations, and body types.

Stephanie Yeboah is among these success stories. She's described as transforming from a wallflower into a forthright woman with a talent for approaching men after using Bumble:

> She'd been struggling with her confidence since she was a teen-ager. That changed when she decided to take control of her dat-ing life and get on Bumble, where she had to approach men. It was scary at first, but she quickly found herself enjoying coming up with questions. It even became a new talent of hers. Before she knew it, she was making moves in all areas of life with courage she'd never felt before.

In a separate page, Stephanie expands on this somewhat patronizing assessment of the role that Bumble plays in her life by telling us about her body struggles and the male rejection she encounters based on her appearance. She also says that while many of her Bumble dates don't amount to much, they have helped her develop an enhanced sense of agency and self-worth. That narrative is more empowering than an endorsement focused on how Bumble helps her get guys.

Thanks to a quick Google search, I discover that Stephanie is a multi-award-winning content creator and author who advocates for body image issues and self-confidence. Her website is gorgeous and I'm a bit stumped about the omission of this information in the Bumble success story page. The dating app isn't mentioned on her site either. Why wouldn't she leverage her success story with an industry leader like Bumble, and why wouldn't Bumble include her own successes as part of their sponsored story featuring Stephanie?

Is she too successful in her life beyond the Hive? The message that users need Bumble to lead them through the dark dating waters is repeated throughout the company website. There the company employs a standard advertising tactic of creating a problem that is solved by the product; it also echoes the altruistic language used in the marketing of apps more broadly, where they're positioned as helpful technologies designed to make life easier. There's an app for that.

But by making dating seem much harder than it may actually be, Bumble is poised to influence ever-more experiences that were not previously ruled by dating apps. I call this "swipification," an example of which is featured in a *Forbes* story by Theo Miller about how bewildered dating app users are when picking a spot to meet. Miller writes, "The dating app Bumble has innovated somewhat in this regard. They offer 'BumbleSpot,' an officially approved array of locations that are safe for meetups and offer ice-breaking activities." The website also features a story called "How to Tell Someone You Like Them."

When I read this, I hear Jennifer Coolidge saying, "daaa-tinng is reeeaaallyy haarrrd." Have we become so dumb that we can't pick a spot to meet up for a date? No, but these examples reveal how dating apps like Bumble are trying to domesticate us by driving home the message that because dating is so hard we should entrust everything to the big yel-low Hive. By surrendering to these companies, however, we may be rooting out some of the unique, random, and diverse aspects of dating that make it what it is – hard, scary, fun, and unique to each person. It also illustrates how ever-more aspects of our lives are becoming digitized. But the world isn't made only of plastic and processors, not yet anyway.

Relying on profit-driven companies to educate us in the ways of dating, communication, and intimacy isn't working out super well for a lot of us. If we go entirely digital will we lose the ability to do romance and interpersonal communi-cation in the flesh on our own? Can these things grow back if we put down our phones or swipe on our own accord in ways that enable us to resist the corporatization of romance?

Hinge

Known as "the dating app designed to be deleted," Hinge is an outlier in the swiping arena. As Maddy Massen writes in *The Tab*, its design is adapted from the Gale-Shapley match-ing algorithm that's been around since 1962 (and earned its developers a Nobel Prize in economics in 2012). Like the other two apps, this one uses an algorithm that tabulates user likes and dislikes, but the registration process is distinct. It features questions designed to get at compatibility and the type of relationship people are seeking, which is not assessed on the other two platforms, although users can put it into their profiles. Good luck getting anyone to read it, though!

As with most platforms, the more users swipe the more information is generated and the more precise the matching process can be. Hinge also has a "dealbreaker" option that further refines the kinds of matches generated because users know upfront what issues or behaviors are off the table for their prospective matches. Smoking, for instance, is a big no for a lot of swipers. Hinge is described on its official website as a company driven by the principles of authenticity, courage, empathy; this straightforward message hits differently than the others. It feels centered and caring, as though our love lives, not just profits, actually matter.

Hinge leverages the role of science in their product development, referring to their researchers and analysts as "love scientists," which is pretty adorable. Hinge is not yet popular in my smallish city, which means there are very few men to choose from. I keep getting matched with Americans affiliated with military bases in nearby Michigan. As much as I love the ding of a new match in the morning, traveling stateside to get my sexy on isn't in the cards.

I manage to meet one Hinge guy for a date. We have dinner at the same local "farm to table" restaurant that I take two other dates to that week. Date smarter not harder! The mojo needle isn't registering as I munch and nod my way through those seventy minutes. What keeps me going as I take long glances around the restaurant – nothing to see here – is one of his profile pics. He's standing calf-deep in a garishly colored plastic pool for kids and snow dusts the ground. I'm not sure if the grimace on his face is a smile or a frozen cry for warmth, but something about it says, "I have the balls to do something a bit risky." However, I never see those gonads and we part ways. Months later I spy him on another app, where he's swiped right on me again. Have mercy.

Many folks I speak with, especially those looking for something more than hookups, prefer Hinge to Tinder, Bumble, and other apps like OKCupid and Match.com. This says a lot about what consumers want and it demonstrates that dating apps can be designed differently; they don't have to follow the standard approach adopted by industry leaders.

Dating App Discourse

Alongside algorithms and product descriptions, the way we talk about dating apps contributes to the "meh." When studying the linguistic tools and symbols used to infuse certain terms with special significance, social scientists use the term "discourse." Breaking down the language and phrases used to describe dating apps can provide valuable insights about how we as a global society are making sense of swipe culture and its impact on love, sex, each other, and tech itself, that big swipe in the sky.

When I describe what discourse means to my students, I usually say that it's concerned with not just what we say about something, but also how we say it. The COVID-19 discourse, for instance, builds upon preexisting terms that convey certain ideas associated with scientific knowledge and popular beliefs. Words like "vaccine," "public health," "contagion," "freedom," and "conspiracy." Australian author and digital wellness expert Joanne Orlando offers another perspective. In *Life Mode On: How to Feel Less Stressed, More Present and Back in Control When Using Technology*, she discusses how we can resist the digital creep into virtually every aspect of our lives. She suggests that we "break up with our phones," which is a cute, effective example that draws upon familiar ideas we already use to combat toxic romantic relationships.

In this section I present six dating app discourses that contribute in varying ways and degrees to the "meh." They represent some of the most common ideas currently circulating in news and social media stories about dating apps, how we use and feel about them, and what they illuminate about our complex and fluid relationship with digital technology.

Privatization

Whether in an Uber on the way to dinner or slumped against a wall somewhere, when we swipe on dating apps we engage in identical behaviors – looking at a small screen in our hand, thumbs poised, the decision-mill turning. However, the solitary nature of this activity can lead to more of us feeling lonely, a trend attributed to the impact of social media in general. This emotional fallout doesn't only affect a few long-toothed people you worked with that summer who still use

Plenty of Fish or kids who grew up with cell phones – it affects millions and millions of us: 323 million ... and counting.

Sociologist Marie Bergström explores some of these issues in her book *The New Laws of Love: Online Dating and the Privatization of Intimacy*. She argues that online dating removes courtship from supportive social settings and places it firmly within the private sphere, where it becomes an individual practice. The move towards privatization isn't exclusive to dating apps, and it could be argued that it began picking up steam decades ago when family structures and living patterns (e.g., individuals living in separate households, away from family) shifted, and the sexual revolution created the possibility for relationships that aren't strictly defined by marriage, monogamy, and men.

However, it's true that most dating app users navigate their relationships alone, and swiping platforms enhance the individualized and corporatized nature of dating. An extreme example of this is that for many people the most enduring relationship they have during their swiping careers isn't with an individual person or people, it's with dating apps themselves. Alison P. Davis writes about this in her humorous, slightly haunting essay in *The Cut* called "Tinder Hearted: How Did a Dating App Become My Longest Running Relationship?" This poignant article captures how heartbreaking it is to spend years of emotional labor and changing up who she is to have an edge on the latest crop of matches only to end up alone.

Another pillar of privatization in the world of dating platforms is data harvesting, which many users probably don't think much about because it's standard fare in our digital universe. Nancy Jo Sales calls this "Big Dating," an apt term that reminds us of the wealth of personal information the apps collect with every swipe each person makes. The amount of information collected is staggering when you consider that the number of daily swipes made on the apps globally could be in the billions. These platforms scoop up our data for free and if users purchase VIP packages, like I regularly do, we are essentially paying them to snatch our data.

Dating Apps Are the Only Way to Meet

It's where everybody is. How else can I meet someone? These dire utterances permeate how we talk about dating apps and modern romance. Inherent in this message is the idea that these platforms are our only choice – the "meh" experience par excellence. We're getting sick of apps, though, and deleting them to meet someone the "old fashioned way" surfaced as a popular Twitter trend in 2021. The comedic memes poke fun at how app-dependent we are and throw serious shade on the dating approaches of the past.

Examples from a *BuzzFeed* article by Angelica Martinez about the Twitter thread reveal the stark generational divide between those of us who date without apps and the folks for whom that scenario is as likely as a fairy tale or horror story. Take your pick!

Deleting all dating apps to meet someone the old fashioned way, in the Garden of Eden
Deleting all dating apps to meet someone the old fashioned way, looking for women to untie from train tracks

Deleting my dating apps because I want to meet someone the old fashioned way (blacked out at a bar)
Deleting all dating apps to meet someone the old fashioned way (standing on a balcony in the summer air, see
the light, see the party and the ball gowns, see someone
make their way through the crowd to say hello)
Deleting dating apps because I want to meet someone
the old fashioned way (in a full-day detention with
others who seem stereotypical but I learn they are
more than just a brain, an athlete, a basket case, a
princess, and a criminal)

I like the camaraderie implied in these messages and how
we're in the grueling swiping trenches together. But I'm not
sure we're entirely lost to the apps because although they
are here, I am too. So, leave the light on, would you? We
have far more than dating apps at our disposal, and this
example raises some important questions about how well, if
at all, are we conveying that message, especially to the gens
born in the digital age.

We Love to Hate Dating Apps

I receive this message from friends who find themselves in
the throes of unwanted celibacy and/or singledom: "I have to
go back on the aaapps. I don't want to. Help." After my own
swiping breaks I feel the exact same way. Staring down the
options on my Google Play account, I can't think of an easier or
more life-sucking way to get the ball(s) rolling. The love-hate
relationships we have with these platforms is central to our
dating app zeitgeist.

This sticky situation is reminiscent of Doublethink, a term George Orwell develops in his dystopic novel *1984* to describe the act of accepting two mutually contradictory beliefs, like "War Is Peace" or "Ignorance is Strength." For our purposes, it's "Dating app culture is terrible but here's how to game the system," which is the title of a 2022 *Cosmo* story by Annie Lord. Next to Elon Musk and Facebook, is there anything we loathe more but continue paying attention to?

Sidenote: In Orwell's novel, there are four government ministries and one of them is the Ministry of Love or "Miniluv." Sounds adorable and kissy, doesn't it? It's actually a place of torture and houses the Thought Police, a secret force that punishes people for thinking negative thoughts about the ruling organization called "the Party." In this dark space, love is used as a technique of control. The same may be true of dating apps, which are also designed by large corporations to govern our feelings, decisions, and behaviors for their own purposes.

No wonder some of us hate them.

Dating Apps Are Bad for Us

Years ago, I wrote this in my field notes: *"It is a toxic cycle of tech over touch and we're suffering ... It's like laminating a flower and expecting it to smell."* It still feels like this sometimes. In the fall of 2022, Tinder "turned ten" and a gush of stories came out about how bad dating apps are to use and how negatively they can impact us emotionally and socially. Most feature wry accounts of failed "Tinderella" and "fuckboy" encounters, but discussions about the distressing prevalence of violence that streams through these platforms are common as well. Also woven throughout many of these pieces is a sense of alienation that many users seem to share.

Social scientists use the word *anomie* to capture these feelings. Anomie refers to the challenges people have when trying to respond to situations where common values are no longer accepted and new ones haven't yet been developed. In these betwixt and between situations, people often feel a sense of futility and emotional emptiness. The idea of dating as disease floats around my head as I reflect on the ways that these apps feed on our work, frustration, and constant surveillance and often give us very little in return for the love dust we expend.

A swipe is like a spin at the roulette table and the odds of winning are about the same. As bad as they sometimes are for me, they're also fun and sexy, something I explore in depth in chapter 5. How have I honed my skills in managing the negative impacts of dating apps? By being cold and calculated, by reducing my worth, and sometimes through luck and intuition, which helps me feel my way into the romantic experiences I crave.

Cyborgs Who Swipe

Technology slips into our cells. We can wear tech and have it inserted under our skin. The bodily rhythms it tabulates dictate what we buy at the grocery store and what fitness programs to join. For a steep price a sex robot can be my guy, and there's even a dating app that uses DNA markers to forecast romantic chemistry, aptly called DNA Romance. To what degree are dating platforms extending what it means to be human? Have we become automated cyborgs who swipe?

This provocative question brings to mind Victorian-era debates about creation and our relationship with machines. According to the brilliant biologist and feminist oracle Donna Haraway, writer of many books including *The Cyborg Manifesto* (1985), we're already assimilated into the technical realm. In an interview with Hari Kunzru in *Wired* in the late 1990s, she says that the link between virtual and real is blurry beyond recognition: "The realities of modern life include a relationship between people and technology that is so intimate it's no longer possible to tell where we end and machines begin."

It might sound scary, but being a cyborg cruising Haraway's world might be kind of amazing. Instead of mindless bots doing and feeling the same thing or taking over humankind, hers is a gender-inclusive place designed to resist male bias in science and tech culture. It invites the possibility of freedom and rebuilding ourselves using technology as we please versus how it's marketed to us.

These ideas allow us to reimagine current debates about technology and how we think about who we are under the digital sky. In her doctoral dissertation, South African anthropologist Leah Davina Junck examines these issues through what she calls "the Tinder prism." She observes that dating apps are embraced as extensions of the self, yet they're also disassociated from daily life as things that are less than "real." Junck concludes that despite the many disillusionments it creates, we use Tinder adaptively and with much determination because it offers us refuge in the realms of both fantasy and reality.

Addiction

Soon into my swiping journey I set a cut-off date because I feel defeated about my often empty bed and because the culture shock of using dating apps is exhausting. These feelings are amplified by my need to document every match, the fails, and the occasionally sizzling encounter. Make it stop! However, I miss the cut-off date and in fact I extend it by a few weeks. Why do I choose to remain on the digital carousel? I've entrusted my romantic future to this app and any minute now the swipe of my life might materialize.

I could miss out by deleting the app. This sentiment makes me cringe, but it's how so many of us feel and it's something the dating app designers bank on. It also aligns with our sugary romance narratives about someone special being just a wish away. The repetitive nature of how we use swiping platforms and the lack of diversity between them can also lead to overuse. Together, these factors keep the swiping game afoot.

Writing about dating apps in the *Toronto Star*, Stefanos Sifandos says, "It's not geared toward the creation of healthy relationships and connections; rather, it's designed to trigger the brain's reward system." In a 2020 story in *HuffPost*, Alison Hodges says the same thing: "Drugs I don't need; even alcohol I abstained from for an entire year. Dating apps? I craved them."

The slide into addiction is one of the ways that we as a global swiping culture allow ourselves to have the wild things plucked from the places where the heat and the heart live. We use them almost mindlessly and while wearing thick skin, like I learn to grow while using dating apps, especially at the beginning. Fieldnotes from my early swiping days capture some of these concerns and observations:

> *Am I addicted to these fucking things? Is there a difference between addiction and dependence? Why am I asking that!? How does it compare with my addiction to alcohol? Like booze, they have been very bad for my mental and emotional health. They restructure how I spend my time and sort of consume me, but the entertainment side of it and knowing that everybody's doing it reduces the embarrassing idea that the addiction is actually a thing.*
>
> *Things I've said to explain why I stay in unsatisfactory or abusive relationships float to the surface from the old cupboards at the end of the hallway: "It's familiar ... it's comfort ... it's better than being alone." But the most familiar feeling is disappointment and being razor aware that I'm lowering myself, communing with men in what feels like an idle chase. It numbs me, just like booze did, and like drinks it is sometimes fun. It offers a place to go, but it's mainly a tunnel to nowhere that keeps turning as I trip over stupid sexts.*

Is There More Than "Meh"?

I return to that fateful afternoon in my office several years ago, when a student tells me that my dating app woes and experiences are "identical" to hers. Equal parts chilling, intriguing, and embarrassing, this statement flips on a very powerful light inside me. It glows long after that young woman goes to Yale for graduate work, after the pandemic, and it's still on as I write this book.

My kaleidoscopic pre–dating app romantic life is one of the main reasons why this light continues to burn. Twenty-something years of wild, cherished, and sometimes painful adventures dramatically impact my sexual evolution and teach me to appreciate a bounty of bodies, cross multiple boundaries, and grow a flourishing garden of erotic knowledge. It's true that once folks get off the app there's room for innovation and creativity, but so many people remain on them and that's a contributing factor behind the repeat experiences that predominate in digital romance.

Reflecting on the "meh" I wonder about the other impacts dating apps have on our lives, not just in terms of hookup culture, ghosting, and the gamification of relationships, all of which are well-researched and written about. I'm thinking about "meta"-level stuff. Intrinsic information that flows through the cultural ideologies and sexual practices that make this blue planet ping with pleasure and more people. Cosmic things like science, the creation of life, and our future as a species may also be impacted by swipe culture.

She Swiped Me with Science

Many researchers who study dating apps say that despite the digital invasion, we still love one another in the same way. What's changed is *how* we find love, sex, and romance, not our biology or anatomical functioning. Doesn't how we meet impact what happens next, in terms of not just love and sex but also meiosis? Not everyone who dates or gets married will have children, to be sure, but given the huge uptick in people meeting on dating apps they are surely impacting how and where we spread ourselves across the globe.

Dating apps haven't been around long enough for us to make definitive predictions about how they may impact the distribution of our genetic material or what relationships will look like in the distant future. But I can't resist pondering their potential impact. And, as it turns out, I'm not alone in speculating how swiping platforms may impact our sexual and evolutionary destiny.

One fact that's well-established in the scientific research, and in my own experiences in the land before swiping platforms, is that dating apps generate an environment for short-term mating practices that is vastly different from that of our hominid past. The dominant message that swiping platforms are not changing our biology is challenged by some scientists who think they might actually conflict with our evolutionary hardwiring. In a 2021 interview by Stephen Fearing in *Swiped*, evolutionary psychologist David Buss says,

> We evolved in the context of small groups ranging from 50 to 150 with limited geographical mobility. You would encounter perhaps a few dozen potential mates in your entire lifetime. We take this small-group dating psychology and transplant it in the modern world with thousands of mates, and it triggers this short-term mating psychology in a way that never would have been triggered ancestrally.

Glenn Geher and Nicole Wedberg, authors of the 2019 book *Positive Evolutionary Psychology*, are also featured in this *Swiped* story. They explain that organic evolutionary processes take a long time to change our anatomical and social functioning: "Our minds are better suited to ancestral, pre-agricultural contexts than they are to modern contexts." Given this, they argue that the pandemonium of choice, huge volume of potential suitors, fast decisions, and immediate intimacy among relative strangers on dating apps is creating an "evolutionary mismatch."

That sounds pretty biology, doesn't it?

Justin Garcia, executive director of the Kinsey Institute and scientific advisor to Match.com, also talks about the mismatch swiping platforms create between who we are and our biological circuitry, which has been honed for success in environments that are nothing like Swipedom. Garcia is included in the Stephen Fearing story above, where he says, "We are engaging ancient biological parts of our behavior, but the platform is novel and unprecedented. With the rise of the mobile dating app, we are in evolutionary unprecedented waters."

Garcia is also featured in Nancy Jo Sales's game-changing 2015 *Vanity Fair* article about the dating app apocalypse. There, he speaks about how dating apps, especially in the heterosexual mating context, are contributing to an unprecedented moment in human history:

> There have been two major transitions in the last four million years. The first was around 10,000 to 15,000 years ago, in the agricultural revolution, when we became less migratory and more settled. And the second major transition is with the rise of the Internet.

Those are some big shoes to fill or whatever folks wore in the olden days when they were just beginning to domesticate our planet. Clogs? Leather wrappings? Dating apps, love them or loathe them, are revolutionizing our culture and what it means to be human on many levels.

Other examples of how swiping can impact us socially and maybe also biologically include the findings of a 2017 article, published in the *MIT Technology Review*, called "First Evidence That Online Dating Is Changing the Nature of Society." The story features Josue Ortega and Philipp Hergovich, researchers who discuss the social impact of meeting people online as strangers: "When people meet in this way, it sets up social links that were previously nonexistent." As they contend, this could lead to greater socio-genetic integration between people because we are establishing connections that are not based on kinship, geography, race, or even class, as often was the case in the past.

Ortega and Hergovich extend their discussion about diversity and new social links by talking about interracial integration on dating apps, which is happening like it never did in the pre-swiping era. They say, "Interracial marriage has long been considered a measure of social distance in our societies, and this is breaking down with online dating." This could, potentially, lead to a more harmonious society. This issue is the focus of a recent Tinder campaign called #representlove that advocated for the creation of interracial couple emojis. Clearly a promotion tool for the company, this example reflects how our widespread dating app use is impacting our society in some pretty high-level and exciting ways.

Age-hypogamous relationships, referring to those between younger men and older women, might also be turning the socio-biological tide of our romantic partnerships. To that end, researchers from McMaster University in Hamilton, Ontario, are exploring the male sexual selection theory, which claims that menopause evolved in middle-aged women because men have not traditionally been sexually attracted to this demographic. As Morton, Stone, and Singh argue in their article called "Mate Choice and the Origin of Menopause," the increase in younger men choosing older women as life partners could eventually push menopause later into the life cycle.

Where do young men find the older women they want? Primarily online and in the palms of their hands. As an "older woman," I can happily attest to the fact that loads of young men out there are eager to connect with women of my generation. Could this impact our reproductive destiny? Possibly, if menopause gets pushed later into the life cycle and adjacent trends among young men who are less interested in starting families than once was the case continue.

Our relationship future might also be impacted by the ways that youthful generations, Gen Zs for instance, perceive sex. They are having less sex than their peers in the past and are not that into hookups or even relationships at all sometimes. These shifts in the romance landscape are discussed in an episode of *The Atlantic* podcast called "How to Talk to People," hosted by Rebecca Rashid and Arthur C. Brooks. A key issue they talk about is that fewer people are finding themselves in a relationship of any kind: "We're not substituting one kind of relationship for another. We're substituting no relationship for relationship."

Relationships and pair bonds as we know them are drifting far from the sandy heteronormative shores that once moored them. Dating is not necessarily or exclusively about mating, and relationships are not always about sex or children, planned or otherwise. Hallelujah, I say! That model only works for some of us. What new waters or islands lie ahead, and how might these new locations change the ties that bind us as a planet? As a species?

Copy, Paste, Now What?

It's now clear Tinder has become the dating air, or maybe the pollution, we all breathe.

– Alison P. Davis

This quote captures our ambivalence about dating apps as well as their omnipotence in our lives. It also hints at being sick of them and sick because of them, a topic that featured prominently in many of the stories, like Davis's, that came out when Tinder "turned ten."

Bro culture and misogyny, the lack of safety features, and the boring nature of Swipelife are often mentioned in these stories. So too is the way we often feel discarded after years of being reduced to pixels and years of chasing people and relationships that rarely materialize in the ways we'd like them to. Less light is thrown on why so many of our experiences are similar and the potential implications of dating apps on our collective sexual and reproductive future. Hence the copy and paste focus of this chapter.

Some people truly enjoy living lives that are nearly identical to those of their neighbors and friends. The carbon copy approach to life can be comforting and reassure folks that whatever they're doing, whether it's buying a particular house or a brand of shoes, they're doing it in a socially validated way. Having shared aspirations and purchasing products that align with the latest consumer trends is something dating apps, like any powerful industry, depend upon and routinely promote. They serve up "meh" through algorithms that match people who look the same, want the same things, like the same foods, and so on.

This raises some perplexing questions about our romantic uniqueness and autonomy. Relationships and sex aren't a pair of shoes or a vacation in Portugal, where everyone seems to be going. Producing generic experiences of intimacy and gendered communication that flatten out our dating diversity, which has long been essential to our survival as a species, is kind of a big deal.

What surprises me is that so few people are sounding the alarm about this aspect of the global uptake of dating apps. There are some exceptions, however. In *The Atlantic* podcast mentioned above, Arthur C. Brooks weighs in on this flattening and how it discounts the need for difference in love as well as partner selection: "Research suggests that romantic love can blossom when people explore their differences – something I fear dating apps often discourage. It concerns me that many of these apps favor selecting romantic partners based on similar traits rather than complementary traits."

Swipe culture is here to stay and exploring how it impacts not just love, but also how we are being governed by the dating app industry is important. Interestingly, although the process of domesticating our approaches to love and experiences of it on dating apps is very new, history reveals that this is linked to a rather well-worn social and economic approach in the arena of advertising that began decades ago. In *Love, Inc.*, researcher Laurie Essig explores the trajectory of love industries (e.g., romance novels and films) over time and why they emerge as especially popular during times of profound stress.

The most famous example is Margaret Mitchell's *Gone with the Wind*, which was a Depression-era blockbuster. Romance offers us an escape but, as Essig argues, this is often a ploy to pull our attention away from global strife and also from making genuine interpersonal connections. That's the irony behind love industries, including dating apps, which are packaged as opportunities for love and happiness, but in reality often manufacture little more than loneliness.

Yet, like most tech products, dating apps are consistently marketed as helpful. The sense of altruism – "there's an app for that" – is part of our digital language and dating app swipe culture is part of that lingo. They are talked about using tropes that symbolize growth in our capitalist society: they are effective, user-friendly, convenient; they offer choice and help us curate our lives. The danger of this is that it can numb us from resisting or being critical of certain aspects of these platforms that we know and feel to be problematic. It can also blind us to the ways that this powerful industry is exploiting our dating labor and data while promoting swiping as normal and useful.

Digital scholar Ben Williams raises these issues, especially in regard to the notion of governance, in a 2015 article about wearable tech, which can be extended to the realm of dating apps: "These devices are augmenting, mediating and governing the ways in which individuals and social groups engage with their own bodies and health." Dating apps are also transforming how we engage with other human beings and how we feel about ourselves in relation to the most fundamental human experiences, those of love, lust, mating, partnerships, and pleasure.

I draw these conclusions not to confirm our role as mindless cogs in the romance machine. They're intended to shake up how we look at dating apps, which have snuck into our lives so quickly and without much critical reflection on our part about their revolutionary impact on society and who we are. I want to shift how the woman swiping on her phone feels when she's crushed under the weight of disappointment and self-doubt. It's not only her playing at romance when she swipes. Lurking in the corner of the room is a whole industry of Silicon Valley dudes rubbing their cold palms together as she does the dating app dance.

As Dan Slater says, "Dating sites, like the behaviors and matches they facilitate, don't come out of nowhere. There is a geek behind the technology. That geek has a vision. That vision is shaped by his unique geek background" (Slater 2013, 193).

However, all is not lost. As consumers and global citizens, we choose which platforms to use and how we use them. There are more fem-forward and gender-inclusive platforms available, mainly in large cities, which isn't the demographic that all of us hit, but the point is that there are alternatives out there. My hope is that this chapter can help us swipe a little savvier and with less self-blame regarding the frustrations that dating apps can inject in our lives.

There are some exciting meta-level outcomes associated with these platforms, too. They allow us to meet people who aren't part of our immediate social, geographic, cultural, age, or racial networks, which may create the conditions for greater diversity across dating communities. They can help us chart new relationship structures, including those between older women and younger men, that reflect shifting socio-sexual and cultural desires related to family structure, having children, and that ever-burning flame of desire. These insights provide something tasty to sink our teeth into as we ponder the future implications of dating apps for sex, relationships, and planetary interconnectedness.

I close this chapter with a nod to a classic research article by famed American anthropologist Clifford Geertz. Called "Deep Drama: Notes on a Balinese Cockfight," it was published in 1972, when I was just beginning to make my debut outside of the womb. A play on the classic pornographic film of the same era, *Deep Throat*, this article is all about drama, which is a key determinant in dating apps and one of the few things that you can count on to keep certain aspects of the "meh" at bay.

Geertz provides a beautifully rich analysis of cockfights and what cocks (the birds not the penises) symbolize for the Balinese villagers he and his wife lived with in the late 1960s. He talks about everything from the male ego to sexualized play between men and women, and how cocks can be used to articulate community tensions related to war, court cases, and many aspects of Balinese life. In identifying with his cock, Geertz says, the Balinese man is identifying not just with his ideal self, or even his penis, but also with what he most fears, hates, is ambivalent about, and is fascinated by – the powers of darkness.

Cockfights are a battle of good and evil, man and animal, and they take place amid the thick smoke of gods and mysticism. His account of how people groom the animals with "abstract sensuality," pass them around lovingly, and feed them special diets reminds me of how we are with our phones, which many of us treat with profound care and even love. We look for them throughout the day, keep them close to or on our bodies, and often say we can't live without them. Recall Orlando's "break up with our phones" example mentioned earlier. We allow them very intimate entry into our lives.

Our mutual and competing love, dependence, hatred, and calculated use of dating apps reflects the diffuse power they have in our lives to do things similar to the cockfight – test fate, find love, perform idealized notions of personhood, express sexual virility and desire, subject an ex to cruel displays of revenge, throw yourself in the ring. Like the villagers, we must, perhaps most importantly, believe in the power of the swipe to change our lives. And we do.

The "deepness" of the play cited in the title refers to porn but also to the incredibly high stakes, morally and otherwise, involved in the cockfights, which, in most if not all ways, cease to be play at all. This is not just everyday risk, it's very far-reaching. In Bali it can reconstitute the political, religious, familial, and cultural order of a community. In our swiping ring, we are ushering in massive changes that are reviled as both banal and epic, and they too may change the world in bigger ways than we know.

This transformative process we are engaged in can reproduce and solidify a host of preexisting social conditions (race, gender, ability). Yet, unlike what we saw in the Balinese example, it is largely devoid of ritual meaning and agreed-upon function. It may be revolution without a manifesto, but it can lead us to a place where reading is not required, where the only text that matters is the thrust of one another and the hot beat of our hearts. That place is love, which is the focus of the next chapter.

FIVE

Love Me Tender

"The words will soon tumble out of my mouth," I say to more than one friend. It's already here, out in the open. Unspoken and unmapped. It fills each pore when I look at him, when I clutch myself under the sheets, when I turn on my computer. It's there when I wear the nonprescription sunglasses he gives me and happily munch the unbuttered toast he puts on my plate. I will eat anything he gives me. I will eat him like the shiny purple eggplant that slides into my peach as effortlessly as someone opening their eyes.

I am saturated with it. L-o-v-e. It has weight and volume, doesn't it? Substances flow onto sheets, towels, and t-shirts that soak it up. It is a substance. It has substance. It's a cosmic membrane that lines our meaty hearts and makes the frantic beats mean something. Love directs the puffy thoughts that glide off rooftops, soar across continents, and wind their way into the people we want. So many arrows shot into the night.

Love works on us in a million ways. It sets off chemical chain reactions and it changes the world. It starts wars and maybe it ends them too. Love is an invitation, but we don't always know who sends the card because it doesn't have a PO number. That's one of the million reasons we love it and loathe it sometimes. It's why we surrender and why dating apps are so popular.

We scroll in the billions as more than blind sheep who wear algorithmic skin and send our data into the swiping universe owned by meta companies. We spend hours looking through pictures of one another because we are ancient lusty creatures who desire. What and who we desire is shifting, thankfully, as the iron lung of heteronormativity loses its charge. How we do it is very different too. How do these platforms change love? Beneath the fit bits and Botox, we are made of stardust, and we want love.

I recently read the memoir Poet Warrior *by Joy Harjo, the twenty-third US Poet Laureate and a member of the Muscogee Nation. Her words catch me in a way that is welcoming and scary. They suspend my spirit and feel like medicine I didn't know I needed. They remind me that I'm still tender and how very important love is, not only of the other but of ourselves. We must remember to care for ourselves. In the prologue, she writes, "Listen now as Earth sheds her skin. Listen as the generations move. One against the other to make power. We are bringing in a new story."*

Harjo speaks about family as a field of stories and love is that way too. This includes the beautiful ones who touch us with their magic and help us grow alongside the imposters that are called love but aren't really that at all. We've all had these dancers slide across the floor of our lives and perhaps also the surface of our palms, which is where many of us first meet. Like a good story, love isn't linear and here lies a stream of tales about love in the time of dating apps that may frustrate, provide a hug, and maybe ignite a new flame in an unexpected place.

The people we take as our own are like ligaments and other connective tissue, but instead of keeping bones and muscle in place they anchor our experiences of love. These powerful things are contained in stories, smells, gifts pushed to the back of the drawer, and in the lessons we'd rather not repeat as we move from person to person. But what about love itself, that oily, luscious thing that slips between bodies and through fingers when we try to pin it down? We spill oceans of ink to understand it while being pulled under its ceaseless tow.

It is the earth and her sisters floating in the milky indigo: moon, sun, stars. It is us.

We travel many places to find and make sense of love. Physical places, but also those cavernous landscapes where memory grows, and we source the courage to develop empathy for the people who stand before us in the mirror and to trust someone new. Love is a portal through which we can twist and reimagine time, space, and sometimes our own bodies. I'm interested in how love cradles itself inside the sizzling moments and the mundane ones, like when we start buying food our lovers like and begin using their euphemisms.

Love is in the jittery phone texts – is the blinking light green or white? It's when he says "see ya" after an intense, sex-filled sleepover. I feel unimportant and casual. But when he calls me by my name instead, it makes me feel equally unsettled – why so formal? Self-defeating talk reverberates in my head as I roll around on the cat-hair-infested carpet. I set my interpretive radar to 11 so that I can morse code the f*ck out of what he says. And what he doesn't say. I fill in the words with my imagination and dusty barrels of shame.

The very act of opening my mouth feels impossible sometimes, especially with people I love or think I might want to. This is vulnerability. It's also how trauma comes back to town, riding in on the old horse of history and relationship patterns that feel obsolete. I'm learning to recognize and resist these things, but I need people, test people, to do intimacy with to know whether or not my self-care efforts are working.

That's where dating apps come in handy – there are millions of us on swiping platforms. Although a sizable portion of folks aren't interested in dating – as many as half of all Tinder users, according to a recent study by Germano Cruz and colleagues in *Cyberpsychology, Behavior, and Social Networking* – most of us are down for some kind of sexual or friendly interaction.

The love I find while swiping comes in many shades, including the cherry red, four-chamber thrusting variety. The kind I fall into. Murky whites and grays also emerge. These colors are not for men or women, they're for me as I diligently carve a path back to myself. Rainbow colors of love show up my inbox, where people share dark and angry feelings about it alongside those that are kind. It's a connective valve that strikes a deep place in us all.

But how do we learn about love in the first place?

Lessons of Love

I'm standing outside the Knox United Church where I attend preschool. Shivering under a black prairie sky, I wait on the steps as my mom plugs the parking meter up the street. My eyes zero in on an infant bird. The small gummy body stays in my hands for a few seconds until I realize that its purple, skin-covered eyes will never open. When she returns, my mom places it on the ground and pushes the curved doors open, spilling an arc of warm light onto my face. We go inside.

This brief moment is etched into our shared history. During the decades of tumult that follow, we often remark, "Remember when we found that tiny bird?" Both so clearly drawn to the sorrowful discovery, perhaps we each felt like that fragile creature. Or maybe we knew, in some deep marrow place, that we would rescue one another someday. Over the years and very much like that baby bird, we kept falling out of the nest. We didn't die, but survival isn't really love.

I remember angrily taping to our fridge a poem I wrote called "Venus de Treena," alluding to the armless masterpiece carved in Parian marble around 100 BC. I'm fifteen years old and feeling very frustrated, maimed even, by my mom's suffocating, fear-driven love. Randomly, the image of dumpling faced Martin Luther pops into my head. In 1517 he supposedly nailed to the Wittenberg church door a list of new rules to counteract the excesses of Catholicism, thus hastening the Protestant Reformation.

Like Luther, I need to make a point. I don't want to be loved like this and I'm not a possession or something to control. My words make no difference, however. We seethe at one another in the hallway or at the back door as I flee to another party with half a bottle of lemon gin in my purse. Under my mom's roof, love is as slippery as an eel. Something to grab hold of one minute and then wrestle free from in another. It never stays still or feels calm, or safe. Neither does she.

How limbless we both are. Women scrambling to be ourselves and care for one another without any direction or support, both struggling under the weight of inherited trauma and the long shadow cast by patriarchal society.

But there are other kinds of love. I think of the women who walk the family farmhouse floors in borrowed slippers and dark, wide-legged jeans. Sitting beside my uncles and my dad, they laugh with one another while I open Christmas gifts. I can see these women walking through sunlit doorways, their hair like halos. They're often kind, interesting, and reveal to me the diversity of what women in relationships can look like. Skinny, make-up free, braless, chubby, bespectacled, foreign, funny, handy around the house, working as gardeners, writers, political thinkers, activists.

I think about them long after we say goodbye after the holidays or on other occasions. How do they spend their days? What does their bedroom look like? How many outfits do they own? What do they do in their spare time? I'm stumped when some of them don't return for the next potluck dinner and begin learning a little about the invisible complexities surrounding love.

Moving across the country to begin first-year university sets in motion a new phase. I leave behind a boyfriend, family, friends, and the small prairie city I've called home for seventeen years. I go to a Public Enemy show – *Fear of a Black Planet* – and become friends with an artistic trio of hippies several years older than me. I fall for one of them but only a few kisses transpire between us. At their place, we drink, draw on the walls, and, nestled on a sea of second-hand rugs, we talk for hours by candlelight. I thrive in this new environment and when reflecting on this fertile time, I think of what feminist artist Georgia O'Keeffe says about cultivating who we are: "If you can believe in what you are and keep to that line – that is the most one can do with life."

During this formative year I also meet a professor who turns my knowledge of love inside out.

Sitting at one of the nondescript tables laid out in four rows of three, I flip through the *Norton Anthology of English Literature*. The translucent scritta paper, also known as "bible paper," feels delicate and I wonder if I'll be able to understand the medieval writings we will be covering. Our professor walks into the room and my stomach curdles. He looks so ordinary and nothing like the feisty Robin Williams who starred in *Dead Poets Society* two years ago.

The professor tells us that we're starting with a short erotic poem. *This* guy, this guy in cheap dress pants and a hospital green short-sleeved shirt with the undershirt visible, is going to read to us about this stuff. Isn't it mainly hot people who know about sex and love? I trace my finger along the curved lines etched into the desk while waiting for him to begin.

Composed around 1595, "The Flea," by John Donne, is essentially an ode to blue balls. It opens with a guy saying to a woman, "Hey babe, it's no big deal to have sex and don't worry, it won't affect your reputation." Then he's jealous of a flea that bites each of them because it's full of their love: "And in this flea our two bloods mingled be." The prof adjusts his glasses and holds the book about a foot away from his face, its pages spilling open like loose linen. He begins reading.

I'm entranced. Each word is vigorously and playfully enunciated, and he walks the aisle with spirit and confidence. He makes that old-ass English sound buttery smooth and delicious, just like Donne intended. How brilliant to use a flea as a metaphor for love, sex, and death. Fleas were everywhere in Europe when this poem was written, causing plague and pandemonium. But to keep writing about sex in a time of mass death and chaos is life-affirming. Maybe also apocalyptic.

I leave the lecture a different person than who I was ninety minutes ago. I rush to his class every week, gleefully entering the galaxies he creates with his voice and his commitment to teaching us about literature as well as life. My favorite is *The Canterbury Tales*, a collection of stories told by pilgrims traveling from London to the Saint Thomas Becket shrine at Canterbury Cathedral. The Wife of Bath, who's hilarious, crass, tough as old boots, and reputed to be a sex worker (red stockings are always a dead giveaway), is the best tale. Indeed, this wise crone pulls from the stars inside herself to tell a tale of women for the ages.

A dashing knight rapes a young maiden and instead of facing the executioner's sword, he's given a year to figure out the answer to a riddle about what women want in life. While traversing the kingdom for clues, he's repeatedly bewildered because the women he meets give different answers: honor, looks, money, sex, remarriage. He's then intercepted by an old woman who has the answer but will only tell the knight if he pledges himself to her, which he does.

She tells him that women want sovereignty over their husbands. The old woman asks the knight to marry her, and he grudgingly accepts. Then, in a series of fantastical events she magically transforms into a beautiful young woman. Partly a patriarchal story of men achieving freedom and pleasure through women, it's also a tale about love as a pledge to women, something solemn and lush that can bloom in the darkest room.

Eighteen years later, while in New York City interviewing for a tenure-track job, I get the word sovereignty tattooed on my back. "That's a big word," the artist says. I nod and smile into the black pleather table as he fires up his machine. From flea to sovereignty. Through the liquid years and the mound of failed relationships that follow, these reminders of love are stored in my cells. I don't dream of marriage and refute the idea that everyone has one true love floating around the planet somewhere. Many people can rewrite our dreams, feelings, and futures in powerful ways.

I want someone to love me solemnly and to show me it's safe to venture out of the trauma cairn that has covered me for decades. Perhaps this is a truly anthropological quest of knowing myself through the other. To discover someone or a few folks who can help me see myself through the love they shine on me. Shards of what I imagine this to be come into view, intermittently, over the years and make many moments gleam. But healing is a slow art form and the love

I aspire to takes a long time to appear. When it does it's entirely unexpected, exciting, and a little terrifying.

Loving Me, Loving You

Martin Chilton, who writes for udiscovermusic.com, estimates that over 100 million songs have been recorded about love. Glorious saccharine emotions are featured in many of these tunes, but just as many describe the pain and sacrifice that often permeates love. Lest we forget that the top love song of all time, according to Google, is "I Will Always Love You." Written by the Smoky Mountain goddess Dolly Parton, this song about how love can become a tear-stained postcard we carry around after leaving someone is something most of us can relate to.

Love is depicted in popular culture as something mind-altering, akin to a drug. This makes sense because love can make us do things we don't always feel in control of and it can also feel mighty, mighty fine. The mothership cluster of goodness in our brains that controls most of our bodily functions, called the hypothalamus, kicks these feelings into high gear by producing dopamine and oxytocin. These are the "feel good" and "love" hormones that are released during intimate experiences like hugging, breastfeeding, and orgasm.

It's no wonder so many writers talk about love in biological terms, as something natural that we're hardwired to do. This is what anthropologist and resident expert at Match.com Helen Fisher tells us in a 2015 *Wired* story by James

Daly: "Love is one of the most basic parts of our brain system ... It's who we are." If love is who we are, I wonder why we are so misguided in its ways.

Must love career through our lives like a roller coaster to be considered true? How do we navigate things from the past that masquerade as love but feel like something else? Can we edit and enhance what we want from love? Yes, we can do this. Black feminist author and activist bell hooks tells us this in her exceptional book *All About Love*, where she says, "When we work with love we renew the spirit; that renewal is an act of self-love, it nurtures our growth. It's not what you do but how you do it."

I am seeking renewal through loving myself and by testing the waters of love for other people. A simple-sounding aim perhaps, but nothing feels harder sometimes. Scraping away the residue of the past and seeing my new face shining through, a face that's sober, learning, still struggling, and happy to be alive. That face, that woman. That's who I'm nurturing; she's what I'm growing as I swipe and dog paddle towards the new people who show up at my door.

My self-nurturing mode is periodically interrupted by a gnawing sense of needing to rein in my frothy sexual desire. A little devil suddenly appears, red and pudgy with a pitched tail and possibly a lit cigarette. It leans into me and whispers, "Mind your appetite, girl. You don't want anyone to know how lusty you are." This pint-sized patriarch in rouge is such a drag! I flick it off my shoulder and instruct my feelings to roam wherever they like.

These overlapping ideas wiggle their way into my fingers as I write sexy and sometimes silly messages to endless numbers of men on my phone. I'm doing it, this work of love and healing, with almost every swipe. Love slides past me like numbers on a roulette wheel. I'm really into a few guys right away and imagine what it will be like to meet their friends, watch them trace their fingers across my inked body, and learn more about their wardrobes. Do they have brown *and* black dress shoes, for instance?

I'm reconfiguring how I think about myself as a healing woman who wants to prioritize pleasure, kindness, and mutual respect in relationships. I do a lot of this work on my own, but straight-talking writers, influencers, and everyday cool people I interact with on social media also impact me, sometimes profoundly. They introduce new toys, kinks, and the wisdom of their experiences. These folks also encourage me to prioritize myself, listen to my feelings, and write about these things in ways that center what I think and what I want to say.

Dating apps and the ways we use them create many problematic social trends related to sexuality, communication, and gender within the realm of modern relationships. Yet they also offer almost endless opportunities to experiment with love, sex, and my healing self, making them ideal places to try on new ways of being intimate. I stumble and swipe my way through meaningless and meaningful interactions without too many harrowing embarrassments.

How does this process of shedding and renewal show up in my dating app encounters? Here are a few heart-shaped examples of what love and things close to it look like as I swipe my way through the digital jungle of men on Bumble and Tinder.

Blue

Blue is a primary color and the most magical in my eyes, which are, you guessed it, blue. It can also be considered a basic color, similar to this guy. Where's the drama or titillating adventure in that? I ask myself this question repeatedly during the four months we date. Is being nice enough to base a relationship on and find some sexy fun? Maybe even love?

Blue is the first Swipedom guy I'm exclusive with, which feels sweet but I'm also a bit wary. The initial sparks aren't super definitive and the idea of being trapped in a boring relationship is awful. It's been a few years since my last real relationship, so why not see how it goes? Plus, people who know Blue consistently describe him as "a great guy," "a good guy," "so nice." How can I lose?

With the amber light of summer streaming through the windows of his basement apartment, we remove the yellow app from our phones. It's official. Deleting apps with partners is a modern courtship ritual that marks the transition from hookup or casual to something more meaningful. It's the second time I engage in this rite of passage and, similar to the first time, it feels nice to be someone's person, but something about it also seems juvenile or make-believe.

I feel caught between what I tell myself I want – a guy, one lover – and the pulsing desires inside me. Uninstalling an app doesn't magically unplug these feelings, at least I don't want it to. I'm not entirely sure what I want and settling for someone just to have someone is kind of tragic to me. However, I smile and go along with the celebration because it aligns with the stories about romance and relationships that are splashed on social media, in movies, and the stories we're told as we grow up.

Later, as my body moves underneath him I look at the wooden carving hanging on the wall and wonder if I can I do this. Can we work on the sex? Of course, but I'm tired of teaching men. When healthy is hard, maybe that's what these confusing feelings are about. I'm adrift inside the learning curve that comes with healing. I grasp at straws, cross all appendages, and hope that my hard-earned self-love and buoyant strength will bring me what I want.

The land of safe relationships is a foreign place that grows amid deep memories and years of patterned living that must recede to make room for the now. Learning to trust the sense of safety that is taking root is also new. So much healing depends on this dance between the inside and out, and those scary choices that don't come with guidelines but offer a way through.

I listen to soft gurgles and the sound of air leaving his mouth. We breathe in unison, but I'm not asleep. His body finds mine repeatedly as he turns and quietly burrows into me. When will he be the spoon? That's what I want, to be taken and to be held, not hung on to. When we join a few minutes later I'm disappointed. Morning is often my favorite. Does this matter? Is there something wrong with me? I finally find a guy who is beautifully kind and cute, and I'm uncertain.

Life is about creation and compromise. It's also about trusting the voice I sometimes try to ignore, the one that speaks the decision I know I must make. I review the tiny list of things we share alongside the pages of differences. I know that being nice isn't enough for me, but I'm fighting with myself to determine if I have the right to believe that.

Women are born into a world that tells us to put others first and that relationships must be long to count. To have a bunch of short ones versus one or two long ones is still seen as a sign of failure and an inability to do commitment or achieve successful intimacy. Why not view it as adaptive and innovative? I say goodbye, and instead of the bitter, shame-ridden drama that cloaked most if not all of my drinking-day breakups, it's an amicable departure. Blue ribbon right here.

Pink

There are many pinks, from the wet rose between my legs to the foamy cotton candy twirled onto a paper cone at the carnival. Both are sweet, like certain parts of this relationship that turns me into something I never thought I'd become: a sugar mama.

I'm intrigued when this gorgeous, very young man replies to my initial message. In our first texts I learn about his world travels and former life as a paramedic, a career pursued by several men I match with. Before Pink and I meet, I gleefully share his profile picture with friends, one of whom says, "If that's the last face I saw before departing this world, I wouldn't mind leaving."

Although seventeen years isn't the biggest age gap in my amorous career, it's the first time I actually date someone that much younger. From the close talking, intentional eye-gazing without looking away, and mutual hotness radar that blows up on the first few dates, I realize it's not an issue for him. In fact, he is particularly interested in older women, including some of the writers and social justice advocates I follow online.

Beyond greedy fantasies about the prospect of physical delight with this hunky man, his awareness of these influencers impresses me at a philosophical level. Cool conversations go an awfully long way in creating as well as maintaining that sparkle. Maybe his insights can help round out my understanding of masculinity, sexuality, and how men experience dating apps.

Sounds great, right? Go team me!

But there's always something and in this case his allegiance to non-monogamy makes me nervous. It's one thing to appreciate relationship fluidity and quite another to experience it, especially when contemplating something serious. I have no clue how to do it. Wistful ideas about me being "enough" for him and also being totally cool with sharing him rise to the surface of my baby poly brain. What kind of sexual advocate am I if I don't practice what I support?

I peruse classics like *Sex at Dawn*, *The Ethical Slut*, and *The Smart Girl's Guide to Polyamory*, and keep coming back to the notion that being jealous of this man's other partners is linked with my compromised self-esteem. Hmmm. It's also the fact that we're sold a particular story about what relationships and, by extension, love and sex are supposed to look like. Two by two is the dominant plot, but our sociosexual worlds have always been much more varied.

It's daunting, but I'm proud of myself for stepping into this alternative landscape. I feel modern and comfortable trying new things on my own and with him. For part of our 1.5-year relationship, I have another partner, which adds some drama and another person to talk intimacy and life with. I like it. Does this mean I don't think about the other women, how he compares or prioritizes us, and what they do together when he can't make time for me because he's with them?

Of course, I do.

We exchange "I love yous" at the three-month mark and he says that his other main partner will remain in the picture. I begin crying. After a very intense and sexy psychedelic trip the night before, I feel like I've been kicked in the stomach and then I feel dumb for feeling that. "I just want to be important to you," I say, and he reassures me that I am. We cuddle in bed and then have sex, which sometimes makes everything better, at least for a little while.

After a few months the years between us seem to matter more and so does the limited amount of time and money he's willing to spend with me. In my experience, cheap folks are often selfish folks and the same is true here. Family pressures and cultural differences are also at play, but fundamentally I'm left to plan and pay for things if we want to do more than watch Netflix at my place. I feel used and silly, but also satisfied a lot of the time.

We break up after a few months, and then get back together during the pandemic because I feel scared and lonely. There's no shame in that. But then the immaturity and distancing are just too infuriating.

My cat Elliott crouches next to the bag that holds his toothbrush, lounge pants, four pairs of socks, three t-shirts, and the expensive slippers I bought him. An inventory of disappointment. These things wait in the darkened closet, like me, for word from the reluctant man. I retreat into Florence Welch, who wrote a square book the color of red wine that beats with brilliance. On one black page sits a golden hand with a bright, blinking eye staring back at me. I think of the tedious, ferocious care that love demands, that we demand as we labor to craft ourselves and the things we hold up as the biggest accomplishment: relationships.

When you break up with someone part of you drops away, like chunks of earth over a cliff edge. It's up to you to figure out how to stretch into things he used to occupy, like the other side of the bed. That frying pan that's too wide, like Joni says in her song "My Old Man." His voice and firm flesh are gone, but the experiences don't simply vanish. Memories take shape in the muscular flutter of the heart or a jolt of anger. They're iridescent. A pretty purple that morphs into the creepy blue of a fly's bodice, or maybe a color that isn't real at all.

We finally talk and there are no lies, just the stated wants of people trying to reach one another from opposite sides of the room. Alongside these tough discussions there are words, always words. What would I do without writing? Part salve and part teacher, they lay like gray lace over the screen. My heart is tender but okay.

I'm impressed with myself for trying this relationship. It takes courage, and I like how I love people. It's not perfect but it's big and generous. I also like how this experience extends my erotic repertoire in terms of certain practices and enriches my sensual approach to life, which spills into how I write and how I teach. I encourage my students to explore themselves with curiosity and compassion. I share my work with them, too, which is an act of bravery and kinship in this Candy Crush world.

Brown

Evoking earth, chocolate, and the sultry coat of the American Quarter Horse, brown is a color that's intimately dialed into the natural world. Musky sandalwood sloshing thickly against the sides of a glass vial where I store salacious memories, this man is like that.

The moment I see him coming around the patio at the back of my building I shriek with delight. This guy is drop-dead gorgeous and his perfect veneer-looking teeth glow when he smiles. I'm gonna jump him. We hug and without thinking I kiss him on the lips. A little surprised, he chuckles and says "okay" in a very cute way that revs me up even more. "Just you wait!" scream my cockles from inside my black G-string.

Some beauty is paired with skill, and some is not. This man is fun in bed, but very focused on himself and what I can do to hasten certain things along. Because this is so common, I take these inequities in stride while welcoming him back, repeatedly. I don't relish entry-level sex, but I'm enamored with his beauty, and feel stoked to have him in my bed. At times our relationship comes close to sexual servicing; however, it's also an exercise in stretching the boundaries of what love-sex-intimacy feels like as well as the purposes it serves.

He shares his past with me: his adventures with other women and his zealous intake of substances that sometimes land him in the hospital. He's vulnerable and lets his feelings out in an aimless yet also expansive way, like water flooding out from under a door. He's trapped by his hulking body, which doesn't always provide the cover he needs to survive as a man without enough resources to make for himself the life he wants. We text every now and then, and it's been years since our last exchange. There are no hard feelings or strong pulls, just two people who still see something of value in one another.

Yellow

Yellow is bright; it is promising. Love can be that way too. It's the prospect of desire, a face in the window looking for a vehicle that might become as familiar as the body driving it. How many times will I sit in the front seat? On the eve of the first date, everything is on the table.

Sixty minutes before he arrives, I do some abdominal crunches on the area rug in my office. My cat Jhona brings his ball upstairs and plunks it down next to me so I can throw it down the hallway. I feel calm and a little uncertain while preparing for the night ahead. I listen to music he recommends and love the dark jangle that floats out of my phone. The singer tells of a suit-wearing devil he saw on the highway, and I think of my mom, who says she saw the devil once. He was decked out in a gray suit and hissed at her from a windowsill. It was when she was really young and, given what she's been through, I believe her.

As the music twangs, my fingers trace the contours of my left foot. I throw Jhona's ball over the banister and hear him scramble on the hardwood floors to retrieve the toy. The furnace hums on and softly fills the room with warm air. The skin on my foot glistens when I apply body balm, which feels like an act of kindness. Given the heart-deflating dating frustrations of late, I'm trying to not get too excited. It is sad to push these feelings away, and I wonder if I'll ever get what I desire. A partner, someone stable, a guy open to taking risks. Hot sex, I want that too.

I remain curious, though. Will he smile wide at me from across the table and hang on my everything? Maybe he won't be enthralled at all. Will he discover the stuffed animal lodged between my pillows? Sometimes I take it out before a date so that if the sheets do get pulled back, they won't think I'm weird. I leave the faux animal tucked into its spot, like a secret to ponder. My stuffie isn't revealed that night, but he does stay over, once.

I haven't had a man sleep beside me for seven months, and although I'm super tired my body has other ideas. It's keeping a vigil of sorts, and my senses are on high alert. I'm on the wrong side of the bed and don't know where the cats are. I'm disoriented. He makes unfamiliar noises, and then gets up to pee. It feels too intimate for two strangers.

We go out for dinner a couple more times, have some great laughs and also a few awkward texts. I mull over the possibility of something more while revisiting his well-designed profile pictures. The guy on the phone seems different than what I imagined. How do we know unless we try? But trying doesn't have to always mean staying, and the lemony sun soon sets on this date.

Green

Green is the color of life, and it symbolizes new things. It's also about growth and is associated with the natural world, where this guy spends much of his time. He is the man in the garden featured at the end of chapter 1, the golden swan smeared with my scent.

When ideas of love come to me, I think about listening to him snore in the twilight hours. I'm a little golden spy under the duvet, basking in his noise. When he plops his arm around me, I can barely breathe. The most casual acts can be supercharged with intimacy. Like when I close my eyes slowly at my cats, who then do the same thing in return. In blindness we trust and bind ourselves together.

His profile pictures tell a story of adventure, athleticism, and a penchant for having fun. Working hard to play hard is highlighted in his blurb, which is a mantra I used to live by. What I don't anticipate is his quietness, which is comforting and intriguing. On our first date he listens intently and shares cool tales of traveling in India, an experience we have in common.

He offers me a ride home, which I greatly appreciate instead of trudging through the wet snow. When we arrive at my place he asks if a hug is okay. Yes! I have to go on my tippy toes to reach to his mid-chest and he chuckles, "You're so tiny." All smiles. Two days later we take a winter walk in the park and exchange more of ourselves.

He's shy, has only one parent, and struggles with some health issues. He learns about my book, my abusive relationship, and how much I love cats. We slow our pace when four deer come into view on the ridge above us, and for a moment it's just six animals looking at one another. They're so marvelous, all legs, wet black noses, and elegance. Five days later he makes dinner at my house, moving through the kitchen with grace and efficiency.

The meal is delicious, and I keep chunks of the French bread in my fridge for months after the date. They're still there. I scour the house for show-and-tell items and settle on a custom bowling ball that's designed to look like the milky way. His beautiful forearms move gloriously as he examines the ten-pound ball. I hear myself gasp, but don't move in for the kiss. Neither does he.

We read one another through layered webs of past relationships, family patterns, and the unknown. This is a delicate task, and we do it carefully. It's only after date number four, when we close down the dim sum place and there is substantial flirting going on, that I make my move. A juicy kiss in the car leads to hours of sweaty exploration, fun, and the sweet stink of sex.

Pacing myself and feeling confident enough to give him space to be himself are among the most important things I learn with Green. Yes, there have been frantic texts to friends, wailing that he doesn't like me because he hasn't been in touch for thirteen hours. But those subside as we grow into what it is we are building together. There's no hurry, which feels like a brilliant discovery.

When friends ask me about his family or past people, I often draw a blank because these are not things I inquire too much about. Letting him unfold himself seems like the right approach and over time he has let some of this information fall into our conversations. I like how it's going and am drawn to him for so many reasons, not only his beauty and fascinating profession, but also because of the way that our vulnerabilities align.

We may not be in the exact same place in our lives, but where we come from is similar and that's a powerful thing to share. So too is the way he shows me that he's thinking of me, which takes the form of texts but more often it's adorable animal videos and links to funky, nostalgic songs on Spotify. If we still had mixed tapes, they would look and sound like the things he sends me. What a precious and thoughtful way to continue planting our love.

Love Mail

Love brings people together and it sparks curiosity. Laying my foibles and never-ending questions bare, with empathy and curiosity, strikes a chord with people of divergent ages, relationship situations, and political leanings. Have you found love? What did it take to get there? Will I ever find a genuine connection online? These are the questions that strangers, colleagues, family members, and friends ask me most often. I get a lot of emails and online messages too, which are a treasure trove to explore and respond to.

Like music or poetry, love is a human dialogue we have in common. The messages and emails I receive reveal how much we care about love and relationships. They also remind me that we don't share our unique, wild, and sometimes crushing experiences enough with one another, which is something many people mention in their exchanges. Most folks who reach out share their stories to connect and to not feel alone. We all need this reassurance and dedicating more time to doing this emotional work together in our daily lives is important.

This is especially true for men, who contact me far more often than women do. Sometimes they're crafty and hit on me, which is mildly flattering, but what I enjoy most is when they reflect on how their dating app experiences impact their lives, their ideas about technology, and their quest for love. It's also touching when they ask for advice and want to talk about the big questions that we all have about love as well as life itself. What does it all mean?

The messages below are mainly in response to my first published article about dating apps, specifically Bumble. As discussed in chapter 3, this article went viral and created a tsunami of misogyny and global interest in my writing. In terms of who the senders are, all but the last three notes are from men, which reflects the gendered breakdown of folks who reach out to me over the years by email, comments on article websites, and on my social media platforms.

Dear Professor Orchard,
I read with interest about your experiences with online dating apps. I just wanted to share with you that my wife and I met through a website called eharmony.com. We met in June of 2005 and got married in June of 2006. We feel that eharmony did a great job of matching us up. They asked 432 questions that seemed to discern how compatible we might be. It was the first marriage/co-habitating for both of us.

My wife is a professor and I'm a priest. I'm sorry that your experience was not that successful, but I did want to let you know that it can be.

I do hope you continue to explore the various internet dating methods as it is something that I have not seen explored much, beyond the description that some are very targeted (eharmony) to the shotgun approach (tinder). I look forward to reading more about your research.

Best regards,

Hi Treena,

I read the Bumble article on the Australian ABC website. I would like to know what hope there is for men like me, separated/divorced 17 years ago, complex issues that I have had, mainly resolved, never really had a relationship since then. I work as a Psych Nurse, met a 72 year old man last year who had been kicked out of home by his female partner. Another guy I met had a conservative Wife (in her 50's) who dumped him and took off with a 26 year old guy. I deal with lots of sad stories in Psychiatry.

Went out with a female colleague yesterday, just seemed to be a friend's thing. Is there any hope for us guys, is it just a "numbers game"? Just turned Hawaii Five O, considering becoming a monk. I have also watched a few MGTOW (Men Going Their Own Way –toxic male separatist group) vids on YouTube which paint relationships in a negative light to say the least. Would love to meet someone have a family (maybe?) settle down and care for each other. Is this possible in this day and age? Can you offer any help or suggestions?

Many Thanks and Happy New Year.

Hi Treena,

Just read your Bumble article, am on the other side of the world in Australia ... the irony is that you will probably get a lot of worthy male attention now! :)) ... tho a bit difficult to believe that you are not single by choice?

:)

Hi Treena:

I really enjoyed your article about Bumble. Hopefully they'll take your suggestions into account and improve the user experience.

I found it very disturbing that some of my gender were abusive to your overtures, despite them knowing the social contract they had entered into by signing up. A real man should never treat any woman like that, ever.

Continued success in career, life and love.

Hi, Treena,

I wonder if you get dates THIS zany way [on Facebook]. Saw your article in the *London Free Press* and I'm writing. I'm also single.... 50, yadda-yadda.... I'm at the Uni quite a bit and you look FAMILIAR....?!?! I might be there Tue 6 PM for a Performance. I WILL be there for sure on Sat 4th @ 2 PM to see X on Piano, she's brilliant. I can also tell you about the "new, chic" social group taking over London; maybe we could do coffee.....?!?!?!

PS I have a buddy that's on Bumble.... where you shake the phone!!! What next!!! Oh, well!!!

See ya!

Hi Ms Orchard

I have read your article on Bumble on the ABC site and am interested in how your journey with online dating as ended or in fact if it ended at all. I am newly divorced after a 25 yr (wow) relationship with 16 yrs of marriage and 2 years later. I live in a city of 300,000 and am a school teacher. I find myself in a precarious position where my social circle has become quite small – centered around my children and work life. I do not want to mix work with pleasure and also do not want to "go out" on the weekend in a hapless search for a partner.

So – I defer to your experience with the dating app Bumble. It was recommended to me by a friend as one that allows the woman to control the situation. I have not tried any app and am very hesitant to put myself in that arena. I worry about my students finding my profile or also my ex-husband finding my information. If you have time, I would appreciate your insights into the experience and the pitfalls of which to be aware should I go down the digital path.

Wow,

I saw a post on Facebook detailing your description of your dating experiences. I've been on an app since last summer after a dating/sex hiatus of 6 years. Along with a ton of amazing counseling over the years, exploration of my own spirituality (unraveling childhood, etc) I am absolutely fascinated with the dating world. I entered the on-line scene with a fair bit of fear and trepidation and am as self aware as I can be navigating this crazy world.

I am not entirely sure why exactly I am emailing you.

But it was inspiring to read about your experience. It's fascinating to me even though I am living it. Partly because with each date I am discovering new things about myself or clarifying my subconscious ideas, but also because it truly inspires me to pursue more of this study. It's quite the circus out there.

Anyways, thanks for sharing. I feel quite separate at times from the larger group of single women on Facebook because I find generally they have still the expectations that men are going to behave in a certain agreeable way. Perhaps I am quite far along in my ideals.

Just super interesting for me.

Good afternoon, Treena
I wanted to say congratulations on your new book chapter about older women and younger men. It's quite courageous to publish such intimate details from your personal life as a professor. I agree with what you say and also like younger men, in fact I married one. Good luck in your writing and I'll look for your book when it's published.

I Am, I Am, I Am

In her phenomenal book *Run towards the Danger: Confrontations with a Body of Memory*, Canadian actor, screenwriter, and producer Sarah Polley writes about encountering and learning to heal from various kinds of trauma. Referring specifically to her prolonged recuperation from concussion, she says "in order for my brain to recover from a traumatic injury, I had to retrain it to strength by charging towards the very activities that triggered my symptoms."

Men cultivate danger, fun, attention, love, and sex, and they're something I run towards. They help silence some of the tangled things inside and can make me feel good as I continue to process old traumas from the past. Like Sarah, who's reconditioning her brain to manage scary things instead of being shut away in a lightless room, I am retraining my brain, my heart, and my way of living. I do this through love, and dating apps help create a deeply valuable pathway to men as well as revised, kinder, different ideas about myself.

Writing is central to recreation. Words bring into being the person who has been waiting patiently to push herself through the cocoon of change into a new reality. There is an embryonic thread between the biology of becoming and its written articulation, both of which are essential to transformation. Writing leads us to the dreams we seek and the things we wish to overthrow, which American poet and public intellectual Adrienne Rich writes about in an essay called "When We Dead Awaken: Writing as R-Vision," published in 1972.

At several points in this essay, she talks about women as monsters. This isn't an abstract reference to the supernatural but, rather, a way of highlighting how women under patriarchy are excluded to the point of not recognizing themselves, including their desires for bodily and sexual autonomy. These monsters are not idle victims, however; they are women like her who actively work against oppressive norms to make lives for themselves that they can be proud of and enjoy.

The brilliant film director Guillermo del Toro speaks about monsters in a similar way in his international traveling exhibit called *At Home with Monsters*. This incredible collection includes rich cultural references to gore, horror, and Frankenstein alongside gorgeous items like mourning dresses worn in Mexico during the Victorian period and a library room devoted entirely to Edgar Allan Poe that features ravens, a bust of the author, and the sound of pouring rain.

The sacred and the familiar are united in this testament to monsters as outsiders who might be closer to ourselves than we'd like to admit. Don't we all feel like we don't belong or don't measure up at one point or another? I see this exhibit weeks after I begin swiping on dating apps, and it makes me think differently about things that I used to be ashamed of. Making friends with the strange things that dwell inside ourselves is part of being human, and it's vital to loving ourselves. We can love our monsters; in fact, we must.

Leave those damn screws in your neck, girl, and learn to love them. Someone else will too.

Chris Kraus, whose radical words open this book, talks about monsters in her 1997 book *I Love Dick*. In fact, she writes about wanting to become a monster, specifically a female monster. In the world of Kraus, these creatures are scientific, inquisitive, and interested in drilling down to the truth of our feelings about ourselves as well as our knowledge of the world around us:

> Female monsters take things as personally as they really are. They study facts. Even if rejection makes them feel like the girl who's not invited to the party, they have to understand the reasons why … Every question, once it's formulated, is a paradigm, contains its own internal truth. We have to stop diverting ourselves with false questions … I aim to be a female monster too.

There is no singular notion, feeling, or account of love. It exists in conversation with sex, intimacy, and relationships. Love is a lens, and it can be used to (re)negotiate the past as well as ourselves.

Love is intimately bound up with the riddle of who we are. Instead of questioning what we know about love and mapping out what we truly want, we often let red roses and albums called *Red* speak for us. This reaffirms what we already know about love and allows us to stay put, often repeating the same patterns until we don't. How do we remake love on dating apps, which are often considered terrible, meaningless, and even violent?

Australian researchers Lisa Portolan and Jodi McAlister explore this question in a 2021 article in the journal *Sexuality & Culture*. They focus on how people navigate love and romance on dating apps, specifically the dominant master plot most of us have been conditioned to see as "normal": you meet someone, you fall in love, you marry, you have children, you live happily ever after.

Although apps arguably offer the best chance to meet someone, they're based on mathematical algorithms and the logic of premeditative strategies, which run counter to the fate-oriented nature of most romance narratives. This leaves many people swiping with a great deal of uncertainty and cynicism, and it's no wonder they describe falling in and out of relationships not only with each other but also with the apps themselves.

This captures our dating app zeitgeist. The apps are used by more and more of us, but we're swiping with chagrin instead of enthusiasm, and there's often very little hope of finding meaningful experiences.

Most of us know that love isn't the driving motivation for every dating app user, nor does it need to be. Replacing the fairy-tale message with something more diverse would do a lot of us good, and although some apps highlight making "friends" and building "social connections," the search for love and finding "the one" remains a pervasive idea within dating app swipe culture.

I think it's useful to remember that everyone on these platforms has a ghoul or two kicking around. This doesn't mean putting up with misogyny or other abuses, but remembering to read the platforms more closely and acknowledging our shared vulnerability can temper the ups and down that come with swiping.

Love is the riotous crotch of religion and it lights a million candles in the dark. We scale mountains to discover, control, and understand the electricity it generates. As much as we buckle under uncertainty, we invite the unpredictable magic of love into our lives time and time again.

When I'm thinking about what love can help us achieve, this Tennessee Williams quote comes to mind: "When we love ... really love ... in any way, we are announcing to the world that we intend to survive." Love is about life, and it can be about even more than surviving, too. It feels exciting and can be a way to say I'm here and I matter. Sylvia Plath wrote about this in her novel *The Bell Jar*, which is where this section title comes from.

"I took a deep breath and listened to the old brag of my heart: I am, I am, I am."

Conclusion

The sticky, sexy, and sometimes sad galaxy of dating apps is a strange and fascinating place. So many planets beckoning to be explored and millions of cold stars glowing with sexy weirdness in the skies we hold in our hands. Ridiculed as juvenile and lamented as impossible to master, these platforms are also critiqued for the sexual violence and swindling that have arisen alongside swipe culture. I experience all of these things, and more.

I stumble into this new landscape anxious and ill-prepared. Every ghosting, gross comment, and hot sexual interlude feels fresh and achingly intense because it's the first time. Add to this my low-key obsession with sexuality and professional chops in figuring out why people do what they do, and the stage is set for a perfect adventure. Each chapter is a glimpse into this frothy story about life inside the dating app cosmos.

Chapter 1 explores how we use selfies to represent ourselves and decode one another. Chapter 2 examines how dating apps are transforming how sex happens and what it means. Chapter 3 flexes on gender inequities that run deep on the Bumble dating app, which is not as feminist as it's marketed to be. Chapter 4 considers design issues and how our global use of identical swiping platforms yields eerily similar user experiences. Chapter 5 is where love rules, all sorts of love, that ancient and powerful pulse that aligns us with other people as well as ourselves.

My beguiling and sometimes agonizing experiences on dating apps transform how I think about the increasingly porous boundaries around sex, dating, gender, and technology. Everything seems to bleed into everything else. Being a sex-positive feminist woman in the digital age feels exhausting and never entirely safe. I'm closer than ever to the remarkable resilience that characterizes how we humans move through the waters of desire and enter love's wilderness.

Ideas, events, emotions, and memories hum and criss-cross this magical space as I write. This story is mine but it's also yours because the heat and worry of love and the intimacy and electric release of sex are essential ingredients of life that dictate how we organize ourselves socially. They direct our future as a species, too. Dating apps are transforming these things in complex ways and despite their ubiquity, few writers have documented their cultural significance.

I return to the question that inspired this book: What do these platforms reveal about sexuality, gender, technology, and the commodification of desire in the twenty-first century? Before sharing some takeaway answers to this question, an update on my dating adventures is in order. Is there anyone special? Do I still clutch the swipe to myself like a fig leaf, to paraphrase Joni Mitchell? What's next for dating and the world of digitally mediated technology?

Dating apps have not graced the surface of my phone for a couple of years. After the first meeting with the man in the garden, I have one more date with someone else and then that's it. To pescatarianize the popular beef-oriented saying about having a steady partner I'm ga-ga for: "Why go out for fish sticks when I've got wild salmon at home?"

Ending this story in a meaningful relationship forged from swiping platforms sort of makes me feel like a traitor. As one person who reviewed my book says, "Tied up with a nice bow, eh?" Aren't they lame, poorly designed spaces where incel and Silicon Valley bros come to gloat and we all have the same outcomes? In many ways, yes. But it would be untrue to conclude that dating apps can't also lead to steamy, wonderful things. No self-respecting scholar leaves out findings that could contradict her hypothesis or the observed trends about a given phenomenon. The truth is messy and so are dating apps, which can't be reduced to a singular label or interpretation.

Will I return to the apps should something in my relationship go awry or we want to shift lanes? Yes, with a great deal of trepidation, but yes. I'm sufficiently armed with the knowledge about how these swiping systems work and know my triggers and fun spots such that the next sojourn should be less of a struggle. Interestingly, although I'm not currently using a dating app, after taking a nice selfie I catch myself saying, "that would make a good profile pic." Swiping experiences permeate my sense of "what if," and the sticky, sexy, sad culture of romance that give them meaning are deeply embedded within me.

Dating apps are central to my healing odyssey. They help release old skins and old ways of relating to other people affected by the tainted lens of alcohol and unresolved traumas. Having said that, it's not easy – the swiping or the healing. In fact, they're both grueling and require hours of work, reflecting, and adjusting to the flurry of things that go on behind the scenes. That's why there are thousands of Pinterest quotes about how difficult change is: you know the ones, they're usually set against the backdrop of a majestic mountain range.

Scale those mountains. Start wherever feels right and begin to climb. No yoni eggs or divine goddess workshops will bring you to where you need to be as effectively as the tenacious, illuminating work of self-care.

Something else that can ease the challenges of swiping is standing up for yourself when folks on dating apps treat you like you're a pixel. You might be surprised what happens when you call someone out. More than a few such men have not only apologized, but they also share their insights on what swiping is like for them. It's not that great on their end either, which is something I'd love to explore in greater detail, possibly in my next book.

Swipe Culture: Love It or Leave It?

Swiping my way into hundreds of conversations with men whose names I'll never remember and some I'll never forget is a little like running the gauntlet. Instead of being surrounded by angry soldiers poised to strike me, I'm trying to make it past the dating app industry on one side, with its tricky incentives and algorithms, and society, with its mixed messages about women, sex, and tech, on the other.

Is modern romance just a vacant swipe? Not always. Let's revisit some of the most compelling aspects of swipe culture, beginning with sex.

Sex

Sex is considered the pearl in the luminescent dating app shell, yet it can be so hard to find. This odd aspect of swiping is linked with how dating is marketed as limitless – there are so many people. Having endless options is framed as part of the fun and good users are supposed to keep busy. The emphasis on swiping versus selecting one or two people to focus on can make decisions that much harder, often culminating in the crippling "grass is greener" mentality where no choices are made and little or no sex is had.

Ghosting also complicates our ability to score on dating apps. It happens to me *so* many times, and yet I constantly wonder where they go and why they vanish like steam into the digital ether. I don't know where they go other than probably on to the next swipe, but I have some theories about why they vanish. For some folks, swiping is for kicks and they're not here to date or have sex, so sexting and even making plans is illusionary. As discussed in chapter 2, these platforms are flipping traditional dating behaviors such that in-person interactions happen much later in the dating game, if at all. This also contributes to the sidelining of sex.

I think some men are afraid to have sex because of the pressure that they may feel to be sexually sophisticated. If you haven't mastered the BDSM art of shibari or been to a kink gathering, what kind of modern sexual person are you?

If you can't make your lover scream from the rooftops every time you have sex you must be doing something wrong. Messages like these can compound the sexting and dating as game behavior. But aren't guys all about sex, though? They're actually not, which contradicts the notion that swiping is just about hookups, especially for men.

Guys want sex and intimacy, but their ability to follow through is constrained by broader factors that seep into the circuitry of dating apps in insidious ways. These factors include things like the changing landscape of masculinity and the lingering effects of #MeToo. An additional factor is porn, which provides few insights into what regular bodies look, sound, smell, and feel like and does not spark our erotic imagination that often. In the absence of quality sex education and the tendency for men to not talk about sexuality or their feelings regularly, they gravitate to places like Porn Hub, where they copy these sexual scripts and think it's sexy.

Changes happening within the heterosexual spectrum also impact how sex shows up, or doesn't, on dating apps. Vibrant new sexual preferences and relationship structures are poking their way through the gray bog of the past. But things like pegging, sex clubs, and non-monogamy can make some straight men feel lost and angry. Many guys I meet say that these issues make talking about sex, let alone doing it, feel risky. These admissions, gleaned during fruitful pillow talk sessions – three cheers for autoethnography – are vital to understanding the barriers to sex that can arise on dating apps. These insights also enrich our knowledge of how straight men feel about sex, which is something many are willing to sacrifice rather than get wrong. These fears and pressures can push us away from one another at a time when we need the special unity of sex, intimacy, and connection more than ever.

Gender

Like sex, gender roles and expression are morphing as traditional power structures begin to fade. Flux spaces hold tremendous potential, yet most dating platforms reproduce gender inequities instead of providing authentic alternatives to them. Look, it's patriarchy in the palm of our hands! This is how it feels when I swipe up against tired old ideas about women and men in my encounters with guys on dating apps. I observe and experience these things most often on Bumble, which is the primary focus of chapter 3.

Touted as the world's first feminist app, on the hetero version of Bumble men must wait for women to ask them out. Initially, I'm all over this unique design and its sleek yellow vibe, which conjures feelings of happiness and hope. But inside the Hive, I'm as disoriented as Alice is when she peers though the looking glass. Instead of a safe, fun place to explore my sexual potential, I feel like a worm wondering around at a robin convention. I'm pecked at, laughed at, and gobbled whole by men who have a hate-on for the platform because of its feminist design.

The misogyny, scary dates, and anti-women tirades I witness and experience on Bumble, where I spend just five months, far exceed anything similar I experience on Tinder, which I've used for over three years. Swiping at the outset of the #MeToo movement likely impacts how men on this app behave, but their animosity and anger cannot be explained by this unique cultural moment alone. It signals something much older, and more deeply rooted.

What I discover from using Bumble is *how* stalled we are in the sexual and gender revolution. I've spent twenty-five years studying sexuality, gender, and health while also engaging in various struggles as a woman and a feminist. How did I not know the extent of this situation? Maybe because my research focuses on other people's lives. Maybe because the black-hearted patriarchy keeps me and millions of other women so busy in the grind of getting by that it can be hard to actually see how cosmically inequitable things remain in terms of gender and power.

My experiences gleaned inside the yellow Hive say scary things about the dark system that circles women, and others, at a close distance overhead. Forty years after women and other folks of my mother's generation held signs saying "Women's Liberation" and "Make Love Not War," I meet men decades younger than me who thump their chests and say they want women in the kitchen. They inherit these ideas socially and express them in various ways through dating apps. These behaviors are buttressed by conservative ideologies circulating in our society about the need to regulate, police, and criminalize women who stray from the patriarchal order, ideologies put into practice by predatory misogynists like Anthony Tate and Harvey Weinstein. Recall the preppy dad who told me to "love it" on a Sunday morning and the scary date in Toronto.

Although using this app is more than a little devastating, it shows me the depths of our contemporary gender divides

and how these divides can be amplified by swiping platforms that don't incorporate the long gender game in their
marketing and design. We deserve more from the dating
app industrial complex than outdated messages of empowerment that feed on rivalry: we need an interface that allows
us to come together equitably.

Technology and the Commodification of Desire

Although dating apps are newish, the way we use them and
the meanings we attach to them as we swipe are influenced
by previous social platforms, gaming culture, and personal
technology more broadly. This helps explain why so many
people swipe when they're bored, to spy on exes, or to find
hotties for their friends instead of dating themselves.

Essentially mini slot machines, the selective wins we score
from the apps tease us into digital dependency. The tailored
corporate and media messages about dating apps depict
swiping as an easy path to romance and social connections.
These messages are typically conveyed through the bodies
of slim, young, white people, and maybe a person of color
thrown into the mix, who may be running along the beach
or laughing in a cool car. It looks like child's play, which
means it's all about fun. It also means don't complain.

These images contradict the tedious, unsatisfying experiences most dating apps users experience at one time or
another. They also make it seem like the companies care
about us – look, they're showing us how fun and easy it
should be – and so when we run into swiping snags we
only have ourselves to blame. This reinforces the notion that

users are responsible for their dating success, which aligns seamlessly with the wellness industry that promotes individual productivity as well as personal sacrifice as essential building blocks to living our best lives.

Don't fall for the giggly photoshopped messages. I'm not saying that it's impossible to find cool people and have some great times; I sure have and millions of us around the world have too. The point is to be smart about not just swiping, but also how you feel when you swipe. Don't blame yourself for your frustrations (unless you're being a dick) and play your hand with confidence and open eyes.

Another thing worth keeping in the back of your mind is that these apps are addictive. Users regularly receive messages about staying active and keeping our dating game strong, that we'll be rewarded with better matches the more we swipe. The emphasis on staying busy echoes social messaging about being successful and being good citizens, both of which are linked to productivity. These values are mobilized by the dating app industry, which transforms intimate relationships into socially validated forms of labor that are bought, sold, and recirculated as aspirational capital within the global economy.

These companies make money from the way we love and express our vulnerability, selling us love in hopeless times. This is a well-worn tradition for romance industries, as Laurie Essig demonstrates in her book *LOVE, INC.*, The cultural trends they endorse surge in popularity amid troubling social moments because they allow us to imagine a better future.

Perhaps most unsettling about the industry's tradition of trading hearts for commercial gain is that the digital dependency it cultivates detaches us from real relationships that offer us human connection, touch, and meaningful interactions. Many studies reveal that frequent social media use can leave us feeling more alone. It also dulls our interpersonal skills, which can make our phones seem like more and more of a refuge. Dating will always be hard, but swiping is not the final stop or the only answer. Put a green pear ring on your finger to signal you're single and wanna meet someone, a cool alternative to swiping introduced last summer. Gen Z and younger users are stepping away from dating apps in other ways, some of which are pretty creative. A popular trend at the moment is to source and study prospective dates on media sites like LinkedIn (professional), Facebook (lame but a trove of old pictures), Instagram (semi-lame, apparently), and Tik-Tok (where billions of people are registered, yes, billions).

This inventive approach is similar to "triangulation," a term researchers use to describe projects that employ multiple data-gathering techniques (e.g., interviews, observations, surveys) to generate a more comprehensive understanding of the subjects being explored. This tactic illuminates the limits of dating app design and showcases the sophisticated sleuthing techniques many folks, women in particular, use to gather additional insights with which they can make more informed decisions about the people they meet online.

Older generations are also going beyond the boundaries of what dating apps offer to maximize their experiences. Facebook groups called "are we dating the same guy in [insert city]?," for instance, are popping up faster than dandelions in the summertime. It's sort of interesting to scroll through picture after picture adorned with red flag emojis, but the stories about women being swindled out of

money, love, and sex are deeply disheartening. I applaud
the women in these groups who are responding to the insuf-
ficient safety nets provided by apps in an effort to take care
of one another.

Newer apps like Hulah may offer women better alternatives. Hulah is described on the Google Play website as

> the dating app that empowers women to take control of their
> dating lives and date only better guys. On Hulah, any woman
> (in a relationship or single) can join and become a ringleader
> and endorse guys for other single women to date. This provides
> real-world accountability for every man on the platform, mak-
> ing it a safer space for women to connect and date.

There's also Chorus, which is one of many matchmaking platforms where "friends swipe for friends" (https://getchorus.co/).
Third-party matchmaking services are seeing a huge come-
back, along with old-school approaches like speed dating. AI
has also entered the dating industry, although in some ways
it's always been there in the form of bots, which plague every
site. Several recent online stories document how AI software
is being used to craft profiles and even conduct conversations for users, especially the mundane opening lines. This
is basically chapter 4 on steroids.

On the Other Side of the Pandemic

What about dating and the pandemic? In the first few months
of our lives during the COVID-19 pandemic, many of us
retreat, while only intermittently swiping. It is a dead time,

that's how it feels for me at least. The desire is there but it's driven by fear instead of fun or the usual angst that comes with meeting new people. Very few dates go well. However, in some parts of the world sex parties rage and people are having masked sex in particular positions thought to reduce the spread of infection. It's reminiscent of the early days of the HIV/AIDS epidemic, when the four horsemen of the apocalypse were galloping towards certain communities very fast, and sex often felt like the only blanket available to keep us warm and to keep us alive.

We are for the most part on the other side of the pandemic, but it hasn't vanished entirely. It's hard to shine a predictive light into the future on that one. At the height of the lockdowns, when no vaccines were yet on the horizon, an image of a box of eels spilling out from my head comes to me during an afternoon nap. When I return to the image later while writing a poem, Medusa appears. Although she's said to have snakes for hair, not eels, I like the uneasy zeal of energy that comes with eels. Like Medusa, they are aquatic survivors.

The electric moon

And then her head exploded
Into a slithering coil of eels
Charged hot and nervous
Amid the viral pause of the planet

The old order tumbles out of her body
Plants push through

Buds taste the grey air
Yet she cannot grow

Why has she come undone?
No cough, no one in the hospital
To moor the isolated woman
Amid the dull waning of the moon

A Feminist Reflects

My encounters with dating apps are changing my life in
ways that keep surprising me. I'm altering my research program at work, and my advocacy and public writing focuses
on digital culture, dating, and relationships. Think of me as
an older, red-headed, inked-up Lucy from the *Peanuts* cartoon strip sitting behind my low-fi sign announcing "The
Doctor Is In."

I want to share my experiences to help others navigate
the swiping carnival and to remind them that they're not
alone in sometimes hating but also maybe needing these
platforms to find the connection they desire. Although the
current roster of dating apps aren't designed to teach us
about love, gender, and sexual desire, I think the 2.0 generation platforms will do a better job at helping us capture the
love/sex/desire we so clearly need.

Other things are changing, too. I fall prey to mean self-talk
much less often and feel more grounded as a strong, sexual, vulnerable, caring woman. Most magical is the energy
wrapped around my voice. It's not golden or perfectly wise,

but it's got glow. I think of influential authors like Melissa Febos, Rebecca Woolf, Heather O'Neill, Sarah Polley, Erin Khar, Lidia Yuknavitch, Tracy Clark-Flory, Cheryl Strayed, Jane Juska, Carmen Machado, and Elissa Bassist, all of whom use their voices to resist the silencing of women in profoundly original and inspiring ways.

We will not be erased, and telling our stories is – and will always be – among the most potent of feminist actions. It's also a way of making our lives on this blue planet mean something worth remembering. We're worth it, each and every one of us.

Sticky, Sexy, Sad: Key Takeaways

These takeaways are like the notes some parents pack in their kids' lunch to remind them they are special and can do lots of amazing things. Nestled in between the celery sticks and the juice box, these are for you <3:

1. Let's invest more in each another and ourselves. Part of this involves listening more closely and asking more welcoming, gentle questions about how we feel. Naming and making friends with our fears and multilayered vulnerabilities is central to the process of grounding ourselves in our selves.
2. We have the right to craft our unique sexual destinies, whether for one night or over a lifetime. This is integral to the human experience and to creating sex lives and intimacies we relish and can grow into on our own or

with partners. Owning this is everything, and we don't need a device to do it. We need sexual courage and support to express ourselves.

3. Let's find creative, inclusive ways to talk about sex, gender, and power that counter the spread of misogyny (and other forms of hatred) and destructive ideas about manhood. Men are scared and scary sometimes, and we need to work together to better understand their vulnerabilities. This is one of the most important ways to help reduce the violence on dating apps and elsewhere.

4. We can collectively push back against the boring, problematic design of dating app platforms that harvest our data for free while getting us hooked on the dark magic of the swipe, which only spits out coins when the algorithm says to. These devices are diluting what counts as sex and are making romance generic, which is the last thing we want.

5. Let's look at swipe culture and the social dialogues about sex and wellness more critically. These industries bank on our submission to and groaning acceptance of the notion that these "terrible but essential" swiping platforms are the only way to meet people. This isn't true. So, let's take charge and make our dating galaxy more satisfying, fun, and dripping with glitter.

No risk, no magic.

Acknowledgments

I've shed many skins while reflecting on the places, platforms, and people I've encountered on the way to get to where I am. Although I enjoyed writing this book immensely, making the shift from academic to public intellectual has been a bit bewildering. Thank you to fellow feminist scholars and memoirists Drs. Tracy Isaacs and Samantha Brennan for providing much-needed encouragement and support in the early days. Big hugs to Dr. Steffanie Strathdee, my long-time mentor in the ways of kicking academic ass and of being a woman living her truth, for help with that most special of creatures, the book proposal. Having a member of your publishing team describe the initial manuscript as a "kitchen sink memoir" was devastating, but it lit an unquenchable fire to hone my craft and learn more about the trade publishing industry.

My entry into the realm of popular writing has been hastened by the gracious input of many other remarkable women, beginning with Dr. Laurie Mintz, who shared resources and recommended expert help. That's how I met Hilary Swanson, a beautiful person, *New York Times* bestselling ghostwriter, and freelance editor beyond compare, who transformed the book's focus and structure. Thank you to Jane Boon, adventurer, technologist, and writer of illuminating erotic novels, whose support and vital insights improved the book proposal. Award-winning journalist, bestselling author, and documentary filmmaker Nancy Jo Sales shared her enlightened expertise as a documenter of popular and swipe culture; her 2021 book *Nothing Personal: My Secret Life in the Dating App Inferno* is the bible of dating app books.

Meeting Dr. Wednesday Martin has been a fun and instructive lesson in how women anthropologists get sh*t done. The plow is not your friend, and neither is the patriarchy. Her impact on my writing and learning to adopt the voice of a cultural critic has been profound. I deeply appreciate your fervent support and that you also took the time to pen the foreword to my book. Also, hugs for being such a dazzling host when I stayed with you and the cats last year.

A chance link on *Publishers Marketplace*™ connected me to Doug Hardy, Gary June, and Tim Moore, my literary agents. As I cheekily said in my first email, "I might write your first feminist memoir." Thank you for guiding me through the nail-biting stresses of proposal development and book submission. Getting to know acquisitions editor Jodi Lewchuk at the University of Toronto Press has been an extraordinary experience. Her razor-sharp professional acumen and lusciously empathetic nature have helped me stretch into new ways of writing and being in the world that are transforming my life. Jodi is also a magnificent writer. Many thanks to copy editor Anne Laughlin for refining my work and providing sage advice on leech removal. To Black Kat Design, I'm entranced with the book cover. I'm also grateful to the anonymous reviewers, whose brilliant suggestions streamlined the book considerably.

Katrina Fortner, the creative conversations about this project we had all those years ago have finally found flesh and form in these pages. Thank you for your insights and enthusiastic fist pumps along the way. Rachel Macaulay brought those ideas to life in my website and, along with writing or co-writing many of the first dating app blogs, she also assisted with social media promotion. I'm indebted to you for your time, patience, expertise, and feminist commitments. To Diane Labuga, my current web-diva, many thanks for your professionalism, timely suggestions, and personal insights as we refashioned the site.

Thank you, Vinita Srivastava, senior editor at *The Conversation*, for asking me to write that article about dating apps and guiding me through the process. It laid the foundation for this book. My sweet friend and distinguished scholar Janice Forsyth first pointed me in the direction of *The Conversation* as a venue for my work. You've cheered me on madly from the sidelines, held the awkward spaces of transition and heartache, and opened the doors to brilliant possibilities I never knew existed. You are medicine to me, and I thank you with all my heart.

To my former high school friend and determined dream weaver Jana Ritter, thank you for helping develop the book proposal, exchanging hundreds of messages and sage advice about dating and men, and never forgetting the side-splitting things that can happen at airports. Robin Wilkins slipped into my life with the grace, generosity, and cosmic serendipity of someone who is not just a friend but also a twin that my soul has always known. Many thanks to Cathy Smith, fellow yogi and listener of sordid dating tales, for your lovely ear and heart.

For decades Kerry Fraser and Chrisa Sikorski have watched me prance, stumble, and regain myself on life's uneven path. Thank you for being there during the brilliant rodeos and also the darkest nights. Heather Richinski, your bubbling enthusiasm has been so uplifting, and when I think of the book, done and dusted, yours is often the first face that comes to mind. A heartfelt embrace to Conor O'Dea, my island muse and long-time compatriot. Fellow traveler of sexual and geographic terrains Melanie Chambers introduced me to writers I'd now be lost without – many thanks for walking this journey beside me. Matthew Strang stands with me too, a one-leg-raised, hot-pink friend of feathery proportions. Thanks also to Susie and Michelle for listening to the storms of confusion and the tender moments while beautifying my hair and my nails.

To quote Nigel Tufnel from the unforgettable film *Spinal Tap*, "eleven, eleven, eleven." That's the feminist frequency humming through Alicia Reitz, a woman who goes way beyond ten in every way possible. Thank you for being so fiery, loyal, funny, and tuned into the nurturing universe that is our friendship. For hugging big and sharing vulnerabilities past and present with grace, thank you Alex Williams. I blow a kiss to Cady Williams: mother, ally, peer, mentor, survivor, and curator of conversations that spiral with wonder, laughter, and wisdom. The bear cub tattoo on my left hand symbolizes my little me, and without my dear counselor Gail I might not have had the courage to get to know her as well as I now do. Thank you for helping me with my life.

My colleagues at Western University and elsewhere have been very supportive, some from a wide-eyed distance and some from across the couch as I struggled to make sense of men, sexuality, and myself. Hugs to Shauna, Tara, Aleks, Elysee, Max, Anita, Rachel, Marie, Marnie, Jenn, Andrew, Chris, Leslie, Anushka, Afshin, Ken, Wendy, Andrea, Chantelle, Alissa, Melissa, Silvia, Anne, and Dianne. Dr. Helene Berman, I deeply appreciate your reading early draft chapters through the eyes of both a mother and a mentor. To Drs. Natalie Rose Dyer and Riki Thompson, you are nourishing sister-scholars. Thanks to Dr. Beniamin Kłaniecki, my darling kin from another generation who enhances my kaleidoscopic world beyond measure. Dr. Emma Rees was the first person to provide feedback on my preliminary ideas for the book; you are a feminist revolution and a cherished friend.

To the students who flutter into my classes and dare to speak their fears and desires, to never say a word, and to keep in touch years after graduation, you are all important to me. Your excitement about the book has brought me profound joy and the necessary courage to carry on in what could be seen as an act of rebellion. Then again, as Guyanese novelist and writer E.R. Braithwaite says in *To Sir, With Love*, "It is our duty to rebel. Not to destroy, but to build upon the grounds laid before us." Build, dear ones.

I'm indebted to my family for loving me through the feral chapters I had to endure before this book could be written. For their vastly different examples of womanhood and independence, for showing me how to do important things, and for their mutual love of cats, I am incredibly grateful to my mom and Sallie. For reading to me when I was small and showing a gentle yet profoundly strong way of being a man, I thank Dennis. For taking me to libraries as well as art galleries and teaching me that children deserve to be considered fully as the important people they are, I thank my dad. To my three sisters, Kathy, Kelly, and Jo Ella, I love you immensely and appreciate the phone calls, collective growth, cute monkey videos, and heartfelt encouragement over the years.

The galaxy of men I encountered on dating apps deserves special mention. I pored over their bizarre, off-putting, and intriguing profiles with the curiosity of Jean-François Champollion, the young Frenchman who deciphered the Rosetta Stone. The ones who wanted to strangle me with their misogyny, the ones who disappeared, and the men with whom I shared both love and the thorny bloom of loss. I extend the sweetest thanks to the man in the garden who so thoroughly rearranged the wild kingdom inside me.

Elliott and Jhona, my furry feline miracles and givers of love that is bigger than I will ever understand. I'd be lost without you and thank my stars and all the others that hang in the sky above that you are mine.

Bibliography

Abrahams, M.H. *Norton Anthology of English Literature.* 5th ed. NY: W.W. Norton, 1987.

Amaruso, Sophia. *#GIRLBOSS.* Edmonton: Portfolio, 2014.

Arbus, Diane. *Aperture.* New York: Aperture Foundation, 1971.

Bassist, Elissa. *Hysterical: A Memoir* New York: Hatchette Books, 2023.

The Beehive. https://thebeehive.bumble.com/.

Bell, Whitney. *I Didn't Ask for This: A Lifetime of Dick Pics.* Traveling art exhibit, 2016.

Bergström, Marie. *The New Laws of Love: Online Dating and the Privatization of Intimacy.* Cambridge, UK: Polity Press, 2021.

Bowen, Eleanor Smith Bowen. *Return to Laughter: An Anthropological Novel.* New York: Anchor, 1964.

Bown, Alfie. *Dream Lovers: The Gamification of Relationships.* London: Pluto Press, 2022.

Brooks, Amber. "20 Dating Sites with the Most Users." June 28, 2023. https://www.datingadvice.com/online-dating/dating-sites-with-the-most-users.

Bumble. "Ambassadors/Honeys." https://thebeehive.bumble.com/ambassadors-bumble-honey.

Bumble. "It Started with …" https://bumble.com/success-stories.

Chan, Lik Sam. *The Politics of Dating Apps: Gender, Sexuality, and Emergent Publics in Urban China.* Cambridge, MA: MIT Press, 2021.

Chaucer, Geoffrey. *The Canterbury Tales*. In *The Norton Anthology of English Literature*, 5th ed., edited by M.H. Abrahams. New York: W.W. Norton, 1987.

Chilton, Martin. "Deconstructing The Love Song: How and Why Love Songs Work." *Udiscovermusic.com*, February 14, 2023. https://www .udiscovermusic.com/in-depth-features/deconstructing-the-love -song-how-they-work/.

Cruz, Germano, Elias Aboujaoude, Lucien Rochat, Francesco Bianchi-Demichelli, and Yasser Khazaal. "Finding Intimacy Online: A Machine Learning Analysis of Predictors of Success." *Cyberpsychology, Behavior, and Social Networking*, July 31, 2023. https://www.liebertpub .com/doi/10.1089/cyber.2022.0367.

Daly, James. "Helen Fisher: In the Digital World, We're All Cavemen When It Comes to Love." *Wired*, August 2015. https://www.wired .com/brandlab/2015/08/helen-fisher-in-the-digital-world-were-all -cavemen-when-it-comes-to-love/.

Damiano, Gerard, dir. *Deep Throat*. Plymouth Distributing, 1972.

Davis, Allison. "Tinder Hearted: How Did a Dating App Become My Longest Running Relationship?" *The Cut*, August 1, 2022. https:// www.thecut.com/article/dating-apps-relationship.html.

del Toro, Guillermo. *At Home with Monsters*. Exhibition, Art Gallery of Ontario, Toronto, Ontario, September 30, 2017–January 7, 2018.

De Ridder, Sander. "The Datafication of Intimacy: Mobile Dating Apps, Dependency, and Everyday Life." *Television & New Media* 23, no. 6 (2022): 593–609. https://journals.sagepub.com/doi /abs/10.1177/15274764211052660.

Donne, John. "The Flea." In *The Norton Anthology of English Literature*, 5th ed., edited by M.H. Abrahams. New York: W.W. Norton, 1987.

Doolaz, Soraya. *Dicture*. https://dicture.com/.

Easton, Dossie, and Janet Hardy. *The Ethical Slut: A Guide to Infinite Sexual Possibilities*. Millbrae, CA: Celestial Arts, 1997.

Emerging Technology from the arXiv. "First Evidence That Online Dating Is Changing the Nature of Society." *MIT Technology Review*, October 10, 2017. https://www.technologyreview .com/2017/10/10/148701/first-evidence-that-online-dating-is -changing-the-nature-of-society/.

Essig, Laurie. *Love, Inc: Dating Apps, the Big White Wedding, and Chasing the Happily Neverafter*. Berkeley: University of California Press, 2019.

Farrelly, B., and P. Farrelly, dir. *Dumb and Dumber*. New Line Cinema, 1994.

Fearing, Stephen. "Side-Swiped: Evolutionary Mismatch and Sex Differences with Mobile Dating." *Swiped*, June 7, 2021. https://www.matingstraighttalk.com/side-swiped-evolutionary-mismatch-and-sex-differences-with-mobile-dating/.

Febos, Melissa. *Girlhood*. London: Bloomsbury, 2021.

– *Body Work: The Radical Work of Personal Narrative*. New York, Catapult Press, 2022.

"Feminist Joins 'Empowering' Dating App – Begs for Return of Patriarchy after Constant Rejection. *Pluralist*, July 29, 2019. https://pluralist.com/treena-orchard-bumble-feminist-dating-app/.

Fleming, V., G. Cukor, and S. Wood, dir. *Gone with the Wind*. Metro-Goldwyn-Mayer (MGM), 1939.

Frank, Jillian. "Pricks in Public: A Microhistory." *Jezebel*, October 26, 2020. https://jezebel.com/pricks-in-public-a-microhistory-1845485535.

Frattaroli, Maelina. "How to Enjoy the Journey More by Eliminating the Word 'Should.'" tinybuddha.com, n.d. https://tinybuddha.com/blog/how-to-enjoy-the-journey-more-by-eliminating-should/.

Geertz, Clifford. "Deep Drama: Notes on a Balinese Cockfight." *Daedalus* 101, no. 1 (1972): 1–37.

Geher, Glenn, and Nicole Wedberg. *Positive Evolutionary Psychology: Darwin's Guide to Living a Richer Life*. Oxford University Press, 2019.

Gionet, Anna. "How Many Swipes Does It Take to Find a Significant Other?" *The Loupe*, February 10, 2023. https://www.shaneco.com/theloupe/articles-and-news/how-many-swipes-does-it-take/.

Goodall, Jane. *My Life with the Chimpanzees*. New York: Aladdin, 1988.

Haraway, Donna. *A Cyborg Manifesto*. London: Macat Library (Routledge), 1985.

Harjo, Joy. *Poet Warrior: A Memoir*. New York: W.W. Norton, 2021.

Henson, Jim, dir. *Labyrinth*. TriStar Pictures, 1986.

Hodges, Allison. "I Was Addicted to Dating Apps. Here's What Happened When I Deleted Them for Good." *Huff Post*, November 5, 2020. https://www.huffpost.com/entry/deleted-dating-apps-addiction_n_5fa32158c5b6f1e97fe67a1f.

hooks, bell. *All About Love: New Visions*. New York: HarperCollins, 1999.

Hughes, John, Ira Newborn, and Tarquin Gotch, dir. *Ferris Bueller's Day Off*. Paramount, 1986.

Joost, Henry, and Ariel Schulman, dir. *Catfish*. Rogue, 2010.

Junck, Leah Davina. "Down the Rabbit Hole: An Ethnography on Loving, Desiring and Tindering in Cape Town." PhD dissertation, University of Cape Town, 2021.

Juska, Jane. *A Round-Heeled Woman: My Late-Life Adventures in Sex and Romance*. New York: Villard, 2003.

Khar, Erin. *Strung Out: A Memoir of Overcoming Addiction*. Toronto: Park Row Books, 2020.

Kirsch, Jen. "Is It Time to Delete Your Dating App?" *Toronto Star*, June 11, 2021. https://www.thestar.com/life/relationships/2022/06/11/is-it-time -to-delete-your-dating-app.html.

Kraus, Chris. *I Love Dick*. New York: Semiotext(e), 1997.

Kunzru, Hari. "You are Cyborg." *Wired*, February 1, 1997. https://www .wired.com/1997/02/ffharaway/.

Layton, Irving. *A Red Carpet for the Sun*. Toronto: McClelland & Stewart, 1958.

Lord, Annie. "Dating App Culture Is Terrible but Here's How to Game the System." *Cosmopolitan*, September 2, 2022. https://www.cosmopolitan .com/uk/love-sex/relationships/a41030063/how-to-use-dating-apps/.

Lui, Claire. "12 Tech Companies with the Best Gender Balance Policies." *The Riveter*, 2023. https://theriveter.co/voice/12-tech-companies -with-the-best-gender-balance-policies/.

Machado, Carmen. *Her Body and Other Parties: Stories*. Minneapolis: Graywolf Press, 2017.

Martinez, Angelica. "'Deleting Dating Apps to Meet Someone the Old Fashioned Way' Is the Latest Twitter Meme, and Here Are 19 of the Very Best Tweets." *Buzzfeed*, June 14, 2021. https://www.buzzfeed .com/angelicaamartinez/deleting-dating-apps-old-fashioned-tweets.

Miller, Theo. "A New Wave of Dating Apps Offer Users a Deeper Level of Compatibility." *Forbes*, June 23, 2022. https://www .forbes.com/sites/theodorecasey/2022/06/23/a-new-wave-of-dating -apps-offer-users-a-deeper-level-of-compatibility/.

Mitchell, John Cameron. *Hedwig and the Angry Inch*. Rock musical with original songs and lyrics by Stephen Trask, 1998.

Mitchell, Margaret. *Gone with the Wind*. New York: Macmillan, 1936.

Morrison, Herb. *Hindenburg Disaster*. Radio broadcast, 1937. https:// www.archives.gov/exhibits/eyewitness/html.php?section=5

Morton, Richard, Jonathan Stone, and Rama Sing. "Mate Choice and the Origin of Menopause." *PLoS Computational Biology*, 9, no. 6 (2013): e1003092. https://pubmed.ncbi.nlm.nih.gov/23785268/.

Mull, Amanda. "The Girl Boss Has Left the Building." *The Atlantic*, June 25, 2020. https://www.theatlantic.com/health/archive/2020/06 /girlbosses-what-comes-next/613519/.

Mussen, Maddy. "This Is How the Nobel Prize Winning Hinge Algorithm Actually Works." *The Tab*, May 20, 2020. https://thetab

.com/uk/2020/05/20/this-is-how-the-nobel-prize-winning-hinge
-algorithm-actually-works-157740.

Nichols, M., dir. *The Graduate*. Embassy Pictures, 1967.

O'Neill, Heather. *When We Lost Our Heads*. Toronto: HarperCollins, 2022.

Orchard, Treena. "Love, Lust and Digital Dating: Men on the Bumble
Dating App Aren't Ready for the Queen Bee." *The Conversation*, July 28,
2019. https://theconversation.com/love-lust-and-digital-dating-men-on
-the-bumble-dating-app-arent-ready-for-the-queen-bee-120796.

– "Bumble Article Comments Indicate the Rise of a Far-Right Feminist-
Backlash." *The Conversation*, September 30, 2019. https://theconversation
.com/bumble-article-comments-indicate-the-rise-of-a-far-right-feminist
-backlash-121652.

– "Reflections on a Date Gone Wrong." *The Chorus*, April 9, 2020. https://
medium.com/the-chorus/reflections-on-a-date-gone-wrong-5ade57a3966d.

– "7 Reasons Dating a Younger Man Is a Smart Choice." *Your Tango*,
September 25, 2020. https://www.yourtango.com/experts/treena
-orchard/want-score-younger-guy-me-too-here%E2%80%99s-seven
-reasons-why.

– "Neither Crone nor Cougar: Navigating Intimacy and Ageism on
Dating Apps." In *Gender, Sex and Tech!: An Intersectional Feminist
Guide*, edited by Jill Fellows and Lisa Smith, 86–100. Toronto:
Canadian Scholars Press, 2022.

– "Virtual Sexual Identities: Embodied Aspirations, Tensions, and Lessons
from the Bumble Dating App (Invited)." In *The Routledge Companion
to Gender, Sexuality and Culture*, edited by E. Rees, 65–75. London:
Routledge, 2022.

Orchard, Treena, and Riki Thompson. "Powerful Women Heading Up
Dating Apps Are Framed as Young and Sexy." *The Conversation*,
October 17, 2022. https://theconversation.com/powerful-women
-heading-up-dating-apps-are-framed-as-young-and-sexy-191403.

Orlando, Joanne. *Life Mode On: How to Feel Less Stressed, More Present
and Back in Control When Using Technology*. Melbourne: Hardie
Grant, 2021.

Orwell, George. *1984*. London: Secker & Warburg, 1949.

Peckinpah, Sam, dir. *Convoy*. EMI, 1978.

Plath, Sylvia. *The Bell Jar*. Portsmouth, NH: Heinemann, 1963.

Polley, Sarah. *Run towards the Danger: Confrontations with a Body of Memory*.
Toronto: Hamish Hamilton/Penguin Random House Canada, 2022.

Portolan, Lisa, and Jodi McAlister. "Jagged Love: Narratives of
Romance on Dating Apps during COVID-19." *Sexuality & Culture* 26
(2022): 354–72.

Rashid, Rebecca, and Arthur C. Clark. "The Complexities of Human Love." Podcast, October 17, 2022. https://www.theatlantic.com/podcasts/archive/2022/10/online-dating-apps-ai-tinder/671762/.

Reynolds, Emily. "Has Tinder Lost its Spark?" *The Guardian*, August 11, 2019. https://www.theguardian.com/technology/2019/aug/11/dating-apps-has-tinder-lost-its-spark/.

Rich, Adrienne. "When We Dead Awaken: Writing as R-Vision." *College English* 34, no. 1 (1972): 18–30.

Ritzer, George. *The McDonaldization of Society*. Thousand Oaks, CA: Sage, 1993.

Ryan, Christopher, and Cacilda Jetha. *Sex at Dawn: How We Mate, Why We Stray, and What It Means for Modern Relationships*. New York: HarperCollins, 2010.

Sales, Nancy Jo. "Tinder and the Dawn of the 'Dating Apocalypse.'" *Vanity Fair*, August 6, 2015. https://www.vanityfair.com/culture/2015/08/tinder-hook-up-culture-end-of-dating.

– *Nothing Personal: My Secret Life inside the Dating App Inferno*. New York: Hachette Books, 2021.

Sifandos, Stefanos. "Why Dating Apps Can Be Harmful to Your Mental Health." *Toronto Star*, September 6, 2022. https://www.thestar.com/opinion/contributors/2022/09/06/why-dating-apps-can-be-harmful-to-your-mental-health.html.

Silver, Shani. *A Single Revolution: Don't Look for a Match. Light One*. San Francisco: Atta Girl Press, 2021.

Slater, Dan. *Love in the Time of Algorithms: What Technology Does to Meeting and Mating*. New York: Penguin, 2013.

Smith, Zadie. *White Teeth*. Toronto: Hamish Hamilton/Penguin Random House Canada: 2000.

Solnit, Rebecca. *Men Explain Things to Me and Other Essays*. London: Granta, 2014.

Stevenson, Allison. "This Woman Turned Her Collection of Unsolicited Dick Pics into an Art Show." *Vice*, April 15, 2016. https://www.vice.com/en/article/ppxjem/this-woman-turned-her-collection-of-unsolicited-dick-pics-into-an-art-show.

Strayed, Cheryl. *Wild: From Lost to Found on the Pacific Coast Trail*. New York: Knopf, 2012.

Tennov, Dorothy. *Love and Limerence: The Experience of Being in Love*. New York: Stein and Day, 1977.

Tinder Pressroom. "Powering Tinder® – The Method Behind Our
Matching." Tinder website, July 11, 2021. https://www.tinderpressroom
.com/powering-tinder-r-the-method-behind-our-matching.

Tinder Tech. "Meet Tinder's Chief Technology Officer: Tom Jacques."
Blog, February 23, 2022. https://medium.com/tinder/meet
-tinders-chief-technology-officer-tom-jacques-a66eab86adb7.

UN Women. "Progress on the Sustainable Development Goals: The
Gender Snapshot." UN report, September 2022. https://www
.unwomen.org/sites/default/files/2022-09/Progress-on-the-sustainable
-development-goals-the-gender-snapshot-2022-en_0.pdf.

Vincent, Norah. *Voluntary Madness: Lost and Found in the Mental
Healthcare System*. New York: Penguin Books, 2019.

Williamson, Ben. "Algorithmic Skin: Health-Tracking Technologies,
Personal Analytics and the Biopedagogies of Digitized Health and
Physical Education." *Sport, Education and Society* 20, no. 1 (2015): 133–51.

Weir, P., dir. *Dead Poets Society*. Buena Vista Pictures, 1989.

Welch, Florence. *Useless Magic: Lyrics and Poetry*. New York: Crown
Archetype, 2018.

Wilder, Laura Ingalls. *Little House on the Prairie*. New York: Harper &
Brothers, 1985.

Winston, Dedeker. *The Smart Girl's Guide to Polyamory: Everything You
Need to Know about Open Relationships, Non-Monogamy, and Alternative
Love*. New York: Skyhorse Publishing, 2017.

Woolf, Rebecca. *All of This: A Memoir of Death and Desire*. New York:
HarperOne, 2022.

Yashari, Leora. "Meet the Tinder Co-Founder Trying to Change Online
Dating Forever: On Bumble, Women Always Go First." *Vanity Fair*,
August 7, 2015. https://www.vanityfair.com/culture/2015/08/bumble
-app-whitney-wolfe.

Yeboah, Stephanie. "How Making the First Move in My Dating Life
Increased My Confidence." Bumble website, n.d. https://bumble.com
/en/the-buzz/online-dating-confidence.

– https://www.stephanieyeboah.com/.

Yuknavitch, Lidia. *A Misfit's Manifesto*. New York: Simon & Schuster/
TED Talk Books, 2017.

Zarinsky, Natasha. "Whitney Wolfe Will Get You a Date." *Esquire*,
November 26, 2015. https://www.esquire.com/lifestyle/sex/
interviews/a39872/whitney-wolfe-bumble-2015-breakouts/.

Index

A Single Revolution (Silver), 144–5
AI (artificial intelligence), 222
algorithms, 142, 145–6, 149–50, 151–2, 154–5
alienation/loneliness, 157–8, 162, 173, 221
All About Love (hooks), 188
Amaruso, Sophia, 107–9
Andreev, Andrey, 106
anomie, 162. *See also* alienation
Arbus, Diane, *Aperture*, 39–40, 41
At Home with Monsters (exhibit by Toro), 207–8
autoethnography, described, 17

baseball metaphor, 72–3
Bassist, Elissa, *Hysterical: A Memoir*, 133
Bell, Whitney, "I Didn't Ask for This: A Lifetime of Dick Pics," 28
Bergström, Marie, *The New Laws of Love*, 158
Brooks, Arthur C., 170, 172

Bumble (app): algorithm, 151–2; alleged feminism of, 8, 100, 109–17, 130–3, 217–18; "ambassadors," 108, 109; beginnings, 106–7; branding and marketing, 151–4; "Bumble Paradox," 116–17; BumbleSpot, 153–4; capitalism of, 110, 116, 154; design/features, 109–13, 114–16, 117; drawbacks, 109–11, 115–17; effectiveness, 111–15, 116, 117; founder, 8, 105–7, 108, 109, 117; Mike the Plumber on, 135–6; popular phrase about, 40; prettiness of users, 135, 151–2; strategies used on, 135; success stories, 152–3
Burke, Tarana, 100
Buss, David, 167

Canterbury Tales, The (Chaucer), 185–6

capitalism: encouraging dependency, 20, 142, 153–4, 160–1, 164–5, 219–21; messaging, 116, 173; operant conditioning, 142, 144, 219; privatization, 157–9; pushing upgrades, 110; role in creating "meh," 142–4, 154, 172, 173
casual sex, 66–7, 69
Catfish (film), 36–7
catfishing, 37–9
Chan, Lik Sam, 144
Chaucer, Geoffrey, *The Canterbury Tales*, 185–6
Chilton, Martin, 187
Chorus (app), 222
communication: with loved ones, 181; sexual, 60–2, 67, 226
Convoy (film), 32
"Convoy" (song by McCall), 32
COVID-19 pandemic: discourse, 157; effect on dating, 49, 86–92, 96, 222–3; poetry on, 223–4
Craigslist (website), 6

data harvesting, 158–9
dating: effect of apps on, 72–3; effect of pandemic on, 49, 86–92, 96, 222–3; key takeaways, 225–6; pre- vs. post-app dating, 72–4, 139; stages of, 72–3
dating apps: algorithms, 142, 145–6, 149–50, 151–2, 154–5; alternatives to, 159–60, 221; branding and marketing, 149–54, 219–20; compared, 149–56; design/features, 73–4, 109–13, 114–16, 117, 148; discourse of, 156–65; diversity on, 150, 169–70, 175; effect on behavior, 173–4; effectiveness, 111–15; enculturation, 61–2; as extensions of self, 163; finding love on, 181, 189–201, 209–10,

213; finding sex on, 66–7, 215–17; influence on human evolution, 166–71; new and lesser-known apps, 36, 154–6, 162, 222; positive aspects of, 213–14; profiles, 136, 146–7; success stories, 152–3, 213; as transforming dating process, 58–9, 72–3; use during pandemic, 86–92; use of AI with, 222; ways used, 8, 71–2, 176, 181, 210, 215. *See also* selfies; *specific apps*
dating apps, darker side of: addiction, 20, 142, 153–4, 160–1, 164–5, 219–21; alienation, 157–8, 161–2, 173, 221; data harvesting, 158–9; dehumanization, 22, 35–6, 57, 147; low benefit-effort ratio, 112–14; "meh," 139, 140–4, 145–8, 156–7, 159, 171–3; operant conditioning, 142, 144, 219; problematic features, 73, 109–11, 115–17, 138–9, 145–6; sexism/misogyny, 59–61, 62, 115, 147, 217–18; un/reinstall cycle, 144–5. *See also* capitalism
dating creep, 148
dating profiles, 136, 146–7. *See also* selfies
dating stories: Bumble, 8–9, 10–11, 121–30; dating websites, 6–9; Fart Guy, 94–5; ghosting, 21–2, 31, 35–6, 71–2, 84–5, 91; Hinge, 155–6; love, 55–6, 189–201, 213; pandemic dating, 86–92; sex, 75–86, 95–6, 125–8; success stories, 152–3, 213; in teens, 14–16; 13 turning-point men, 24–57; Tinder, 21–2; Toronto men, 74–5; in twenties, 68–70; younger men, 79–82, 95–6
dating websites, 6–8
Davis, Alison P., 158, 171
De Ridder, Sander, 94

"Deep Drama: Notes on a
Balinese Cockfight" (Geertz),
175–6
dick pics, 27–30, 43, 53, 60–1
"dictures," 27–8
digital creep, 47, 157
direct messaging (DM), 148
diversity, 150, 169–70, 175
divorce, 12–13
DMs, sliding into, 148
DNA Romance (app), 162
Donne, John, "The Flea," 184–5
Doolaz, Soraya, 27–8
double standards, sexual, 77

eharmony.com, 202
Elite Singles (website), 7
Elo rating system, 151
enculturation, 61–2
Eros, 93
Essig, Laurie, *Love, Inc.*, 173
evolution, effect of dating apps
on, 166–71

Facebook, swindling on, 45–7,
221–2
Febos, Melissa, 16
feminism: of author, 103–5, 131,
134–5; backlash against, 98–9,
100–1, 102, 118–20, 218; Bumble
claims of, 8, 100, 109–17,
130–3, 217–19; described, 102;
explaining need for, 134–5;
#GIRLBOSS, 107–9, 116, 131;
women as monsters, 207–8.
See also sexism/misogyny
"Feminist Joins 'Empowering'
Dating App" (Pluralist),
118–19, 120
"First Evidence That Online
Dating Is Changing the
Nature of Society" (Emerging
Technology from the arXiv), 169
Fisher, Helen, 143, 187–8

"Flea, The" (Donne), 184–5
Frank, Gillian, 28
Frattaroli, Maelina, 66

Gale-Shapley algorithm, 154–5
Garcia, Justin, 168
Geertz, Clifford, "Deep Drama:
Notes on a Balinese Cockfight,"
175–6
Geher, Glenn, 167–8
Gen X era, 12
Gen Z, 112, 170, 221
gender: inequity, 77, 102, 207–8,
217–19; roles/stereotypes, 58–9,
77, 81, 92, 215–16. *See also* men;
sexism/misogyny; women
ghosting: app responses to, 36;
examples of, 21–2, 31, 35–6,
71–2, 84–5, 91; reasons for, 35, 84
#GIRLBOSS, 107–9, 116, 131
#GIRLBOSS (book by Amaruso),
108–9
GIS technology, 73–4
Gone with the Wind (Mitchell), 173
Grindr (app), 26

Haraway, Donna, 163
Harjo, Joy, *Poet Warrior*, 179
Hergovich, Philipp, 169
Hinge (app), 154–6
Hodges, Alison, 164
hooks, bell, *All About Love*, 188
"How to Talk to People" (*The
Atlantic* podcast), 170, 172
Hulah (app), 222
Hysterical: A Memoir (Bassist), 133

"I Didn't Ask for This: A Lifetime
of Dick Pics" (Bell), 28
I Love Dick (Kraus), 208
"I Will Always Love You" (song
by Parton), 187
inclusivity/diversity, 150,
169–70, 175

"industrial masculinity," 58
intermittent reinforcement. *See*
   operant conditioning

Jacques, Tom, 149
Jones, Jasmin, 144
Junck, Leah Davina, 163

Kirsch, Jenn, 145
Kraus, Chris, *I Love Dick*, 208
Kunzru, Hari, 163

Life Mode On (Orlando), 157
limerence, 42
loneliness/alienation, 157–8,
   161–2, 173, 221
love, 178–210; in art and culture,
   184–6, 187; author on, 178–86,
   188–9, 201–2, 209, 210;
   biological aspect, 187–8; finding
   on dating apps, 181, 189–201,
   209–10, 213; healing trauma
   through, 207–8; polyamory,
   193–4; Portolan and McAlister
   on, 209; stories of, 55–6, 182–4,
   189–206, 213. *See also* sex
love bombing, 46, 47
Love in the Time of Algorithms
   (Slater), 142, 174
Love, Inc. (Essig), 173
love industries, 173
"Love, Lust and Digital Dating"
   (Orchard), 118–20, 202–6

male sexual selection theory, 170
manosphere, 101
mansplaining, 102–3
Martin, Wednesday, 95–6
Martinez, Angelica, 159–60
masculinity, 57–60
Massen, Maddy, 154
Match.com, 7, 143
"Mate Choice and the Origin of
   Menopause" (Morton et al), 170

McCall, C.W., "Convoy" (song), 32
McDonaldization, 143–4. *See also*
   capitalism
men: dick pics, 27–30, 43, 53, 60–1;
   male sexual selection theory,
   170; masculinity, 57–60; sexual
   pressure on, 215–17. *See also*
   gender; sexism/misogyny
Men Explain Things to Me (Solnit),
   102–3
menopause, 170
#MeToo, 100
Milano, Alyssa, 100
Miller, Theo, 147, 153–4
misogyny. *See* sexism/misogyny
Morton, Richard, 170

New Laws of Love, The
   (Bergström), 158
non-monogamy, 193–4
#notallmen, 100

older women, 80–1, 95–6, 170
online aggression, 28–9, 42–7,
   60–1, 148
operant conditioning, 142, 144, 219
Orchard, Treena: academic
   background, 10; Bumble use
   stats, 113–14; chat with Mike
   the plumber, 134–7; childhood
   and adolescence, 12–15, 182–4;
   feminism of, 103–5, 131, 134–5;
   fieldwork in India, 104–5, 140;
   first attempts at online dating,
   6–9, 10–11; flirtations, 64–5,
   68; getting sober, 6–7; on love,
   178–86, 188–9, 201–2, 209, 210;
   "Love, Lust and Digital Dating,"
   118–20, 202–6; poetry, 76, 223–4;
   preferred "type," 58; relationship
   with technology, 4–6; zodiac sign,
   58, 140. *See also* dating stories
Orlando, Joanne, *Life Mode On*, 157
Ortega, Josue, 169

Parton, Dolly, "I Will Always
    Love You," 187
patriarchy. *See* sexism/misogyny
phones, 157, 176
Poet Warrior (Harjo), 179
Polley, Sarah, *Run towards the
    Danger*, 206
polyamory, 193–4
pornography, 148, 216
privatization, 157–9. *See also*
    capitalism
profile pictures, 23–4. *See also* selfies
Psyche, 93

Rashid, Rebecca, 170
#representlove, 169
Rich, Adrienne, "When We
    Dead Awaken: Writing as
    R-Vision," 207
"ritual of transition," 73
Ritzer, George, 143
Robinson, Mindy, 119
romance industries, 173
Run towards the Danger (Polley), 206

Sales, Nancy Jo, 147, 159
sapiosexuals, 40
selfies, 21–63; defined, 23; dick
    pics, 27–30, 43, 53, 60–1;
    importance of on dating apps,
    23, 56–7; insights revealed in,
    24–5, 33–4; masculine displays
    in, 57–8; 13 selfies, 24–57; types
    of, 25–30, 37, 57–8
servitization, 143
sex: casual sex, 66–7, 69; Eros
    and Psyche myth, 93; finding
    on dating apps, 66–7, 215–17;
    pornography, 148, 216; sexting,
    72, 148; stories of, 75–86, 95–6;
    125–8. *See also* love
sexism/misogyny: anti-feminist
    backlash, 98–9, 100–1, 102,
    118–20, 218; on dating apps,

59–61, 62, 115, 147, 217–18;
    gender roles/stereotypes,
    58–9, 77, 81, 92, 215–16; of
    male researchers, 104–5;
    mansplaining, 102–3; online
    aggression, 28–9, 42–7, 60–1,
    148. *See also* feminism
sexting, 72, 148
Sifandos, Stefanos, 164
Silver, Shani, *A Single Revolution*,
    144–5
Slater, Dan, *Love in the Time of
    Algorithms*, 142, 174
sliding into DMs, 148
social media, 44–7, 148, 221–2
Solnit, Rebecca, *Men Explain
    Things to Me*, 102–3
swipe culture: defined, 4;
    discourse, 156–65, 173; learning,
    61–2. *See also* dating apps
"swipification," 153–4

Tame (app), 36
technology: defined, 5–6; human
    relationship with, 157, 162–3, 176
Tennov, Dorothy, 42
Tinder (app): algorithm, 149–50;
    beginnings of, 106; branding
    and marketing, 149–51;
    inclusivity efforts of, 150, 169;
    #representlove campaign, 169;
    tenth anniversary of, 161–2,
    171; Tinder U, 150–1; ways
    used, 8, 181
"Tinder Hearted" (Davis), 158
"Tinder prism, the," 163
Toro, Guillermo del, *At Home with
    Monsters* (exhibit), 207–8
toxic bro culture. *See* sexism/
    misogyny
trauma, 3, 181, 206–8, 213–14
tree photo, 48–9
triangulation, 221
truckers, 32

unsolicited dick pics (UDPs), 27–30, 43, 53, 60–1

Wedberg, Nicole, 167–8
"When We Dead Awaken: Writing as R-Vision" (Rich), 207
Williams, Ben, 173–4
Williams, Tennessee, 210

Wolfe Herd, Whitney, 8, 105–7, 108, 109, 131–2
women: as monsters, 207–8; older women, 80–1, 95–6, 170; saying "no," 132–3. *See also* feminism; gender; men

Yeboah, Stephanie, 152–3
Yuknavitch, Lidia, 16